Evaluating School Programs

CORWIN
PRESS

The Corwin Press logo—a raven striding across an open book—represents the happy union of courage and learning. We area professional-level publisher of books and journals for K-12 educators, and we are committed to creating and providing resources that embody these qualities. Corwin's motto is "Success for All Learners."

Evaluating School Programs

An Educator's Guide

Second Edition

James R. Sanders

CORWIN PRESS, INC.
A Sage Publications Company
Thousand Oaks, California

For information:

Corwin Press, Inc.
A Sage Publications Company
2455 Teller Road
Thousand Oaks, California 91320
E-mail: order@corwinpress.com

Sage Publications Ltd.
6 Bonhill Street
London EC2A 4PU
United Kingdom

Sage Publications India Pvt. Ltd.
M-32 Market
Greater Kailash I
New Delhi 110 048 India

Printed in the United States of America

Library of Congress Cataloging-in-Publication Data

Sanders, James R.
    Evaluating school programs: An educator's guide / by James R.
Sanders. — 2nd ed.
        p.   cm.
Includes bibliographical references and index.
    ISBN 0-7619-7502-0 (cloth: alk. paper)
    ISBN 0-7619-7503-9 (pbk.: alk. paper)
    1. Educational evaluation—United States—Handbooks, manuals, etc.
I. Title.
    LB2822.75.S26   2000
    379.1'58—dc21   99-050853

This book is printed on acid-free paper.

00   01   02   03   04   05   10   9   8   7   6   5   4   3   2   1

Corwin Editorial Assistant: Kylee Liegl
Production Editor: Denise Santoyo
Editorial Assistant: Cindy Bear
Typesetter/Designer: Janelle LeMaster
Cover Designer: Oscar Desierto

CONTENTS

ACKNOWLEDGMENTS

No book is the product of a single person, and this one is no exception. I want to thank Dr. Richard Jaeger at the University of North Carolina at Greensboro for requesting the first edition of this book as part of his project with the Georgia Department of Education. Dick was very supportive and a wonderful critic and editor as the first edition took shape.

Now, nearly 10 years since I completed work on the first edition, it has become obvious to many people that the book needed to be updated. I want to thank Gracia Alkema and Robb Clouse at Corwin Press for keeping after me to complete this second edition. This edition could not have been done without the supportive environment of the Evaluation Center at Western Michigan University and a sabbatical leave during 1998-1999 granted to me by the university. In particular, I want to thank Mary Ramlow and Barbara Wygant for their support on the production of the book.

Finally, I want to thank my wife, Sue, and children, Jamie and Jennifer, for tolerating my long absences while sequestered with my work on the fourth floor of Ellsworth Hall at WMU.

It is great to be surrounded by such wonderful people.

—James R. Sanders
Kalamazoo, Michigan

ABOUT THE AUTHOR

James R. Sanders is Professor of Education and Associate Director of the Evaluation Center at Western Michigan University. He received his master's degree in educational research from Bucknell University and his PhD in educational research and evaluation from the University of Colorado. He has served as a visiting professor at St. Patrick's College (in Dublin, Ireland), Utah State University, and the University of British Columbia. He is coauthor of *Educational Evaluation: Theory and Practice* (1973), *Practices and Problems in Competency-Based Measurement* (1979), *Educational Evaluation: Alternative Approaches and Practical Guidelines* (1987), and *Program Evaluation* (1997). He is author or coauthor of numerous articles, monographs, and technical reports in the area of program evaluation. His articles have appeared in *Review of Educational Research, Educational Researcher, Educational and Psychological Measurement, Journal of Educational Psychology, Journal of School Psychology, New Directions for Program Evaluation, Evaluation News, Educational Technology, Journal of Research and Development in Education, Educational Measurement,* and *American Journal of Evaluation.*

Dr. Sanders has served as director or codirector of training institutes in evaluation for the American Educational Research Association, the American Evaluation Association, the Association for Supervision and Curricu lum Development, and the Western Michigan University Evaluation Center. He has served as a member of the board of directors for the Evaluation Network and the American Evaluation Association and on standing committees for the American Educational Research Association, the National Council on Measurement in Education, the National Science Foundation, Phi Delta Kappa, Independent Sector, and the United Way of America. He has directed research and evaluation projects funded by the U.S. Department of Defense, U.S. Department of Education, National Science Foundation, and several state agencies. He has consulted with numerous school districts, private industries, instructional businesses, government agencies, research and development corporations, community agencies, and major universities. From 1988 to 1998, he served as chair of the Joint Committee on Standards for Educational Evaluation, a coalition of 16 professional organizations concerned with the quality of evaluations done in education. He was elected by the American Evaluation Association to serve as President-elect in 2000, President in 2001, and Past President in 2002.

INTRODUCTION

The Purpose of This Guide
and How to Use It

This guide is intended for use by teachers and administrators in elementary and secondary school systems to help them evaluate their school programs. Evaluation is a complex process, and there is always the danger of oversimplification in a guide such as this. Please remember, evaluation is not a mechanical process; it is a human endeavor, and it carries with it all of the complexities and challenges of any human undertaking, including education.

There are two things above all else that one should remember about evaluating school programs. First, not everyone will see the program in the same light, and it is important to be informed about how those around you view it—its purpose, its approaches, who is involved and excluded, its costs and trade-offs, its accomplishments, its short-term and long-term future, and other things of interest to those who care about and are affected by the program. Second, one must always consider three aspects of good program evaluation—communication, communication, and communication. As long as you listen and respond, share information, discuss your intentions and obtain feedback, clarify expectations, provide clear and useful reports in a timely manner, and maintain an open evaluation process, the evaluation seas should be smooth.

This guide was written to provide basic program evaluation principles and procedures to aid educators in planning and conducting evaluations of school programs. Examples will help the reader to develop competence and confidence in program evaluation. Beyond this guide, however, indispensable experiences will be gained by undertaking evaluations and sharing your experiences with a nearby group of people with whom evaluation issues can be discussed. In addition, there are other evaluation resource materials that go into greater depth on many of the topics covered here. It is not possible to provide here all of the detailed coverage of evaluation topics that some would like. For this reason, references to more advanced or specialized resources are provided (see Resource A and References).

This is a general guide that can be used to help plan any school program evaluation. The general principles in this guide are based on the advice of Daniel Stufflebeam (1969), who suggested that we must always attend to five tasks when conducting program evaluations:

- Focusing the evaluation (see Chapter 2)
- Collecting information (see Chapter 3)
- Organizing and analyzing information (see Chapter 4)
- Reporting information (see Chapter 5)
- Administering the evaluation (see Chapter 6)

This guide will take you through the five tasks of school program evaluation, providing examples along the way. Use the guide as a reference book; it should not be read as a novel and then discarded. As my colleague Richard Jaeger has said, program evaluation does not need to be complex or inordinately time consuming. It does not require extensive technical training. What it does require is a *desire* to improve one's school, a *willingness* to work collegially, careful *attention to detail*, and *basic knowledge* of how school program evaluations should be carried out. This guide provides the last of these key elements.

1

WHY EVALUATE
YOUR SCHOOL PROGRAMS?

Successful program development cannot occur without evaluation. Program evaluation is the process of systematically determining the quality of a school program and how the program can be improved. How good is the program? How do you know how good it is? Is there room for improvement? What should be improved, and in what ways should it be changed? Some of the best evaluation occurs in response to questions that teachers and other school personnel ask about their professional practices. A true mark of a professional is the desire to continue to develop his or her effectiveness. The evaluation principles provided in this guide provide a means for improvement and a way of documenting results so that others can learn from one's successes and failures.

Evaluation gives direction to everything that we do when changing and improving school programs. It is the process used to identify student needs. It is the process used to set priorities among needs and to translate needs into program objectives or modifications of existing objectives. It is the process used to identify and to select among different program approaches, organizations, staff assignments, materials and equipment, facilities, schedules, and other structuring choices in order to build a program that has a high likelihood of success. It is the process used to monitor and adjust programs as they are implemented. It is the process used to determine whether a program is resulting in desired outcomes and why the outcomes are as they are. It is the process used by outsiders to determine whether a program should be supported, changed, or terminated. It is the process used to judge requests for resources to support the program. In short, evaluation is an essential part of the improvement of school programs. It should underlie all changes and reforms. Without evaluation, change is blind and must be taken on faith.

BENEFITS OF
EVALUATION

The payoffs of program evaluation are benefits to school staff and the children they serve. For example, as a result of sound program evaluation, benefits that can accrue to students might include improvement of educational practices and procedures or development of support materials to eliminate curricular weaknesses. Benefits to teachers might include recognition and support for teachers associated with a good program or help in choosing the best curriculum materials. Benefits to principals might include direction in setting priorities for school improvement or the identification and justification of needs for new programs.

The process of evaluation involves two basic acts: (a) gathering information so that decisions will be informed and supportable, and (b) applying criteria to the available information to arrive at justifiable decisions. The process is done systematically and openly, so that others can follow along and all can learn. It is recorded in reports or other documents so that the steps in a decision process about a program can be traced and, when necessary, the results can be reviewed and communicated clearly and accurately. Evaluation findings are reported in writing so that learnings can be shared and made available for future use by others.

FORMAL
VERSUS
INFORMAL
EVALUATION

The evaluation process differs in important ways from the day-to-day personal decisions you make. When you evaluate items on a lunch menu, you do not systematically conduct an analytical study; you do not carefully collect data, analyze it, and report it; you do not explicitly describe the criteria that you are using to make a selection. You just do it. It is highly subjective and not open to public review and debate. One set of values applies. The results are not written up for future use or for sharing with others.

The evaluation of school programs frequently involves a much more rigorous process, because the decisions being made can affect many others —perhaps even the well-being of the next generation. Many perspectives need to be considered and standards must be met. Formal reports are prepared and made public. This is what we mean by formal evaluation.

What should be evaluated in schools? The following chapter presents an initial inventory of things that deserve evaluation. It also provides a process for identifying what to look at when evaluating a school program.

2

FOCUSING THE EVALUATION

It is not sufficient to state that evaluation can and should be a part of all school improvement activities. If responsibilities for evaluation are to be made clear, if evaluation findings are to be used, and if activities contributing to the evaluation are to be coordinated, you need to identify the specific elements of the school system that are to be evaluated.

One school district created the following list of school functions that might be evaluated:

POSSIBLE FOCAL POINTS FOR EVALUATION

1. *Program needs assessments:* to establish program goals and objectives
2. *Individual needs assessments:* to provide insights about the instructional needs of individual learners
3. *Resource allotment:* to provide guidance in setting priorities for budgeting
4. *Processes or strategies for providing services to learners:* to provide insights about how best to organize a school to facilitate learning
   a. *Curriculum design:* to provide insights about the quality of program planning and organization
   b. *Classroom processes:* to provide insights about the extent to which educational programs are being implemented
   c. *Materials of instruction:* to provide insights about whether specific materials are indeed aiding student learning

d. *Monitoring of pupil progress:* to conduct formative (in-progress) evaluations of student learning

e. *Learning motivation:* to provide insights about the effort and persistence of learners

f. *Teacher effectiveness:* to provide insights about the effectiveness of teachers in aiding students to achieve goals and objectives of the school

g. *Learning environment:* to provide insights about the extent to which students are provided a responsive environment in terms of their educational needs

h. *Staff development:* to provide insights about the extent to which the school system provides the staff opportunities to increase their effectiveness

i. *Decision making:* to provide insights about how well a school staff —principal, teachers, and others—makes decisions that result in learner benefits

j. *Community involvement:* to determine the extent to which community members can aid in the decision-making process of the school

k. *Board policy formation:* to provide insights about the extent to which the board is using its authority to communicate its expectations to the staff

5. *Outcomes of instruction:* to provide insights about the extent to which students are achieving the goals and objectives set for them

GETTING STARTED

WHERE DOES ONE BEGIN?

The evaluation of a school program usually begins when someone or some group (usually teachers) has a concern about the current program. The principal might initiate the evaluation and get a group of faculty members to take the lead. Or a grade-level or department committee could initiate the evaluation. However it starts, those doing the evaluation should plan to meet as a group to consider, as a first step, the following questions:

1. Why do you want to evaluate the program? What led to this decision? What is the purpose of the evaluation?

2. Who will use the results? How will they use them? Who else should be involved in the evaluation and see the results?

3. What is the program? What does it include? Exclude? Is it this year's program, last year's, or next year's that we will be evaluating? At what grade level? As implemented by which teachers? Is this the first time the program has been evaluated?

4. How much time and money do you have for the evaluation? Who is going to do it? Have you talked with others about the evaluation? Are they in support?

By listening to the responses of your coworkers, you can form a concept of the type of evaluation that is needed. A *formative evaluation,* which is conducted internally by staff who are working in the program, is one type. Its purpose is to gather feedback on aspects of the program that are undergoing review and possible revision. What is working well and what is not? What needs fixing? Is there a need for "midcourse corrections?" The evaluation is not intended for outsiders. This is the type of evaluation associated with most school improvement work.

FORMATIVE
EVALUATION

Another type of evaluation, *summative evaluation,* usually is motivated by questions from outside and requires accurate responses to questions that outsiders pose. Decisions about replacements, major overhauls, awards, or other accountability decisions often are the end results of summative evaluations. Other individuals and groups typically are involved beyond the program staff.

SUMMATIVE
EVALUATION

GETTING SOME STRUCTURE FOR THE EVALUATION

After the questions listed in the above section have been answered, a decision should be made about proceeding with the evaluation. If it looks as if no one will use the results or the evaluation cannot be done well, you should question the logic of moving ahead.

When you do plan to move ahead with an evaluation, however, there are certain decisions that will need to be made. A discussion of each of these decisions follows.

A basic decision is determining who will coordinate the evaluation. Important considerations are whether these people have the time, the program expertise and credibility, the concern or interest, and the leadership and organizational skills necessary to coordinate the evaluation. Select carefully, for this is a critical decision that should not be taken lightly.

SELECTING A
COORDINATOR

Once an evaluation group has emerged, decisions need to be made about who the evaluation is for. Typically, in-house evaluations are done for the teachers who will be making changes to improve the program. On the other hand, one can ill afford to ignore certain groups or individuals. In an evaluation of a science program, for example, certainly all teachers who teach sci-

STAKEHOLDERS

ence should receive information about the evaluation and, often, should be asked to participate in it. The evaluation group may also want to involve interested parents and school board members, local community leaders and employers, or local educators with expertise in science education (e.g., someone from a university, someone from an intermediate school district, or the district science coordinator if your school district has one). Each individual or group who has an interest in the quality of the science program is called a *stakeholder*. These stakeholders have different perspectives and values when it comes to science education. Their values are worth considering seriously in an open evaluation process, and the results of evaluation could be shared with them if you think doing so would make a difference.

CLARIFYING WHAT IS TO BE EVALUATED

Another set of decisions is needed to get a clear sense of what is to be evaluated. For example, the concept of "hands-on learning" in science has been touted as an essential part of science education. Closer inspection of what one means when the term *hands-on* is used, however, will reveal a wide variety of conceptions; only some of these have proven to be effective, whereas others have little educational value. One can only evaluate clear and accurate descriptions of whatever aspects of the program one has chosen to study. Aspects of a program being evaluated that should be clarified include the following:

- What grade levels are involved?
- Which courses and teachers are involved?
- What is the basic organizational structure of the program? What are its major components and activities?
- How many students are involved at each grade level, and for what amounts of time?
- What resources (human, materials, time) are consumed in the program?
- What is the curriculum design for the program (scope and sequence)?
- What needs are being served by the program?
- Have there been evaluations of the program in the past? If so, what did they find and recommend?

DESCRIBING WHAT IS TO BE EVALUATED

The best way to get a clear idea of what is to be evaluated is to *observe* the program in action, talk to *(interview)* other staff, and *read* documents about the program (e.g., curriculum guides, lists of objectives). Once you have a clear sense of what is to be evaluated, it is a good idea to write it down, so that others will know what you are talking about and so that you will have a record of the program as it once was in case it is changed while you are evaluating it. When changes occur, as they often do with programs, you will want to redescribe the program as it unfolds.

To achieve clarity about a program, evaluators often make use of a *logic model* to describe the program. In Figure 2.1, a program logic model is used to describe the following components of the program:

Figure 2.1. A Program Logic Model

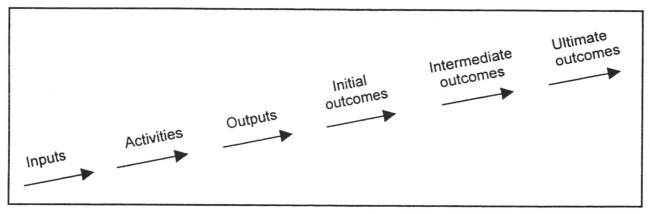

SOURCE: Reproduced from United Way of America, *Measuring Program Outcomes*, 1996, p. 34. Reprinted by permission, United Way of America.

- *Inputs* describe the resources (fiscal and human) needed to run the program, as well as facilities, equipment, books, materials, and other essential ingredients.
- *Activities* describe what you will be doing in the program—the scope and sequence of activities, a timeline, and assigned personnel who will be conducting the activities.
- *Outputs* describe the numbers associated with the program—numbers and demographics of students, number of contact hours, number of classroom and home assignments and time involved in each, number and types of tests and work products, and student/teacher ratio.
- *Initial outcomes* describe the expected student changes that will occur after each activity (e.g., each class). How should students be different from before the activity?
- *Intermediate outcomes* describe the expected longer-term student changes that will occur after a lengthy engagement in the program (e.g., at the end of a semester or year).
- *Ultimate outcomes* describe the vision you have for students who have successfully completed a program of study. This is the ideal. To what extent have they developed as you had hoped?

When developing programs, evaluators often start with the end—the ultimate outcomes or vision—and then work backward to design a program that will get students to that end. Intermediate outcomes and initial outcomes become checkpoints or benchmarks so that progress toward the ultimate outcome can be assessed and midcourse changes can be made if needed. Activities and inputs can be planned as the *means* for reaching the intended initial, intermediate, and ultimate outcomes. A program designed in this way lends itself quite readily to a testing program keyed to expected outcomes.

AVAILABILITY   A final set of decisions relates to the resources and personnel available to
OF RESOURCES   the evaluation. The amount of money, time, support personnel, and exist-
                   ing data that are available will influence the complexity of the evaluation.
                   You can do only so much with limited resources. You need to be realistic.
                   Knowing the resources available to you will help you plan a feasible pro-
                   gram evaluation.

To review, then, the early decisions that must be made are as follows:

1. Who will do the evaluation?
2. Who are the stakeholders in this evaluation?
3. What is to be evaluated?
4. What resources and personnel are available for the evaluation?

After you have addressed these decisions, it will be time to develop a
list of evaluation questions that will guide the program evaluation.

Illustrative Case Study (Part 1)

Before moving on, let's look at an illustrative case application of the mate-
rial that we have covered. Although fictitious, this case is like many faced
by building teachers and principals. Its purpose is to show how the evaluation steps could work in a real school setting. First, a scenario is presented,
and then we will apply what has been discussed so far to the scenario. This
illustrative case will be continued through the remainder of this guide. As
each step in the program evaluation process is discussed, we will return to
this case to examine how the discussion could be applied.

SETTING OF THE   Lakeview City has a population of just over 50,000 people and is located
CASE STUDY   midway between two major metropolitan areas, each about 200 miles away.
                   Lakeview City is the county seat and is the largest town within 100 miles. It
                   has diversified industry, including a major chemical plant and the
                   farm-machinery division of a large national manufacturing company. It is
                   also the home of a 16,000-student state university, which until 1968 had
                   been a state teachers college. The town is about evenly split between
                   white-collar professionals and blue-collar workers. Unemployment is
                   fairly stable at about 4.9%. The school district is recognized as one of the
                   better ones in the state, in part because of its ability to recruit the best gradu-
                   ates of the local university and in part because of strong interest in educa-
                   tion from a good cross section of the town's population. There are about
                   8,000 students in grades K-12. The school district has six elementary
                   schools (grades K-5), three middle schools (grades 6-8), and two high

schools (grades 9-12). About 60% of the high school graduates go on to higher education, with the remainder taking jobs or going into the military. The school dropout rate is low; approximately 2% of entering high school freshmen fail to finish high school.

The state has recently begun statewide testing in science in grades 4, 8, and 11. Last year, for the first time, Lakeview City students at all three levels scored poorly on the test that was given. Although the rest of the state also did poorly, the school board, parents, principals, and teachers of Lakeview City all agreed that this was no excuse. In the absence of a districtwide plan to improve science education, several teachers and the principal at Johnson Elementary School began talking about their ideas for their elementary science program. They each had pet projects that they wanted installed in the curriculum—one was interested in groundwater, another in space, a third in computers and technology, and yet a fourth in industrial applications of science concepts (e. g., engineering). Because all of the projects were important but it was impossible to do everything the teachers wanted, the principal, Mrs. Goss, suggested that a systematic look at the needs of their students and the extent to which the school's present curriculum was meeting those needs was in order. "Then we can see what we should do to improve our science program." The group agreed and also decided to talk to each teacher in the school about doing an evaluation of the science program during the coming year.

In a faculty meeting at the beginning of the year, Mrs. Goss announced that the science program would be evaluated during the year in order to get direction for improving it. The evaluation would be done by a steering committee of interested teachers, possibly with some outside help. Any teachers who wanted to serve on the steering committee were invited to volunteer, and the first meeting of the steering committee was scheduled to be held after school the next Monday. Six teachers volunteered; fortunately, they were evenly split between grades K-2 and grades 3-5.

Mrs. Goss met with the steering committee on the following Monday and reviewed the purpose of the evaluation. "Although we are concerned about the state test scores," she said, "there are several of us who also feel it is time to review and revamp our science program. It has been so long since it was systematically evaluated that none of us remembers when it was last done. Mrs. Cooper, here, has been a primary teacher in this school for 22 years, and the only evaluation she is aware of is what was done by the last textbook selection committee when it was asked to select a science text for grades 4 and 5. Otherwise, each teacher has been doing her or his own thing! We want to use the results of this evaluation to look at our science program in grades K-5 and to see how well we fit with the middle school and high school programs. Are we preparing our children to meet the demands of the science program in later grades?"

At that moment, Mr. Henry, who teaches at the fifth-grade level, spoke up. "I agree that we ought to prepare our kids in science for later grades, but

I also think we should look at their needs outside of school. Are we kindling an interest in science that will last them a lifetime? Are we encouraging girls and minorities to consider careers in some aspect of science? Are we alerting our students to current issues in science, such as toxic waste in the environment and global warming?"

Miss Radisson, a kindergarten teacher, added, "I agree, but we are also killing a natural interest our children have in science topics by our emphasis on rote learning of definitions, names, and dates. Those textbooks are killing us!" Mr. Sanders, a fourth-grade teacher, replied, "We stick to the textbook because that's what we've been told to teach! Besides, most of us have not had any preparation for teaching science. What do we know that the experts who wrote our texts don't?"

At this point, Mrs. Goss broke in and said, "I think we're getting ahead of ourselves. We all agree there is a need to look carefully at our science program and perhaps some related issues. I am going to depend on you to do a careful evaluation and report your findings at a faculty meeting in the spring. We will rely on you to give us direction for years to come. Mr. Henry has been to two National Science Foundation workshops and has taken several summer science workshops at the college. He has also had a course in program evaluation as part of his master's degree. For these reasons, I have asked him to coordinate this evaluation. We have a little money to cover incidental expenses, but check with me before you spend anything. Does anyone have any questions before we break?"

Mr. Henry asked the committee to hold meetings on Mondays after school for the science evaluation study, at least for the month. The members all agreed and departed.

IDENTIFYING THE EVALUATION QUESTIONS

Evaluations answer questions about strengths and weaknesses of a program from a number of different perspectives. You can ask how good a school program is from the perspectives of key stakeholders such as the faculty, who teach in it; parents, who have certain expectations; or employers, who have to live with its products. You can also ask how good a program is according to how well it meets its objectives, how well its students perform on normed tests, or how well it matches a "model" program as defined by the profession (e.g., for science programs, the National Science Teachers Association [NSTA]) or professional literature (e.g., on effective schools, or on "what works" as published by the U.S. Department of Education). All of these are legitimate ways to evaluate a program, but they can result in different conclusions. To get the most informed look at a program, it is usually necessary to draw from each of these approaches.

Unfortunately, the simplest approach to evaluation may not result in the most informed decisions. In this sense, evaluation is like a jeweler holding up a gem to view. By twisting and turning the gem at many different angles, you get different perspectives of its strengths and weaknesses. A simple, quick look would not result in the same conclusions as a thorough examination. In program evaluation, the lives of students, staff, taxpayers, and others are affected by the results. Final decisions about school programs are too important for simplistic evaluation. It is important to be thorough, and the selection of the questions to address in the evaluation is the way to ensure a thorough program examination.

How is the selection of questions accomplished? Easy. Start with a blank worksheet like that presented in Figure 2.2. You are going to fill in the first and second columns (usually it will require several copies of the worksheet to list the most critical questions).

EVALUATION WORKSHEET

Begin talking to key stakeholders you have identified (teachers in the program and perhaps certain parents, employers, or a science consultant). If they were going to look at the science program, for instance, what are the most important things they would look for? What are the characteristics of a good science program from their perspective? How would they know a good one if they saw it? Ultimately, what is their vision of a student who has successfully completed the program? By keeping careful notes of their responses, you should have a good initial list of candidate questions for the evaluation. Of course, you will not be able to address every question thrown at you, but you should come up with a select list of questions that will be essential from the perspective of the stakeholders.

HOW TO IDENTIFY EVALUATION QUESTIONS

Teachers in the program may ask whether the text, curriculum materials, and lab exercises are up to date and consistent with state and NSTA guidelines. Parents may ask what is expected of a student at the end of a grade level in terms of science knowledge, skills, and values. They may also want to know how well their children are being prepared for college, jobs, or national exams. A school board member may ask about the need for additional or fewer secondary-level courses and may be concerned about costs of the program. Stakeholders will help you to focus on the important questions.

You could also plan to compare your program against some existing model or ideal program. The characteristics of a model science program, for instance, could come from standards supplied by your state department of education, from the effective-schools literature, from NSTA or the goals for the year 2061 established by the American Association for the Advancement of Science (AAAS), from the federal "what works" publications, from the evaluation criteria used for accreditation, or from certain "lighthouse" programs that have been identified as being exemplary. You could look at these sources and pull out the characteristics that your program should have. Use your fellow teachers and others who are key people to help you do this so that major stakeholders have a voice in the selection of evaluation questions.

Figure 2.2. Evaluation Information Collection and Analysis Worksheet (Blank)

EVALUATION QUESTIONS	WHY THE QUESTION IS IMPORTANT	INFORMATION NEEDED TO ANSWER THE QUESTION	WHEN AND HOW THE INFORMATION WILL BE COLLECTED	DATA ANALYSIS AND INTERPRETATION PROCEDURES

Finally, you could plan to call in an outside program-area expert, if one is available to you, to indicate what an outside expert might look for in an exemplary program. Add what the expert tells you to the list of questions you have already started.

Next, the teachers doing the evaluation should meet to shorten the list of evaluation questions if it is too long to be workable. The second column of Figure 2.2 will help—if you cannot explain why a particular evaluation question is important, you have to wonder why it is even being addressed. Looking beyond the importance of the question, you can reduce the list by considering who would be upset if the question were dropped, whether the information already exists, and whether it is feasible to try to get an answer to the question.

NARROWING DOWN THE LIST OF QUESTIONS

Concentrate on the most critical questions for your program evaluation, and then fill in the first two columns on the worksheet.

You have just finished focusing the evaluation. Basically, you have done the following:

1. Clarified the evaluation purposes
2. Clarified what is to be evaluated
3. Identified the evaluation questions to be answered

Illustrative Case Study (Part 2)

The next Monday found the science program evaluation committee meeting after school. Mr. Henry had sent a reminder memo to all committee members, so everyone was there. Via a separate memo, he had also invited all teachers to join them. Everyone on the committee had lots of questions and ideas about how to proceed. Mr. Henry called the group to order, noting that he was glad to see everyone but was disappointed that no other teachers were interested in joining them. Miss Radisson reminded him that the science evaluation was not the only game in town: A language arts committee was planning a proposal for a revised remedial reading program, the at-risk committee was meeting, a group was working on a new gifted-and-talented program for the school district, there was the new senior-citizen volunteer program, and so on. "This is a busy place," she reminded him. Mr. Henry agreed. "You're right. We have our priorities, but we have to keep in mind that others have theirs. This will be important to remember when we ask for some of their time and when we try to enlist their interest and support for our recommendations."

Mr. Henry took a piece of paper out of his pocket. "Let's review two things at this meeting. First, let's make a list of who might have an interest in improving our science program, and then let's decide who will contact each group or individual to see what questions they would like us to address. We can then narrow down the questions to a reasonable list that will guide our work this year." Having read *Evaluating School Programs: An Educator's Guide,* the committee members understood the importance of getting multiple perspectives about what to look at in the science program. It was not just the steering committee's program, it was everyone's, and they had to be careful not to ignore the concerns of others.

After some discussion, it was decided that Miss Radisson (grades K-2) and Mr. Henry (grades 3-5) would talk individually with each of the other teachers in the school to ask them what they would look at if they were asked to determine whether the science program at Johnson Elementary School was a good one or a poor one. Mrs. Cooper, a first-grade teacher, agreed to get on the phone to the Academic Boosters, a group of parent volunteers interested in the quality of the education their children were getting at Johnson. The Academic Boosters would be asked to contact at least 30 parents to determine their expectations, especially related to student outcomes. The list of parents was one Mrs. Cooper would give them. The list represented a good cross section of grade levels of enrolled children and social classes of families; it was one that Mrs. Goss had used on occasion to get parent input on school issues. Mrs. Cooper would ask the Academic Boosters for the information by next week.

Mr. Sanders and Miss Jefferson were both taking a course at the university and volunteered to do some library work for next week. One would look for program goals and objectives developed for elementary science programs by NSTA and AAAS. The other would conduct a computer search for recent literature (within the past 2 years) on characteristics of good elementary science programs. They would also ask the director of the science education center at the university for copies of publications on "what works" in science education.

Mr. Williams, a fourth-grade teacher, volunteered to contact a school board member he knew to see if he could get a reading on school board interests. He also said he would get the school's state science test results and identify the areas that seemed to be the weakest at each grade level.

The following week, all committee members came to the meeting ready with their lists of evaluation questions. Mr. Henry listed the questions and where they came from on poster paper as they were read. He combined questions that were getting at the same thing. In total, 28 questions were listed.

Mr. Henry then said, "Are we missing anything? Has some aspect of our science program not been addressed?"

Miss Radisson spoke up. "No one has asked how much has been budgeted for the science program at Johnson Elementary School. This certainly has implications for what we do."

Figure 2.3. Evaluation Information Collection and Analysis Worksheet (First Two Columns Completed)

EVALUATION QUESTIONS	WHY THE QUESTION IS IMPORTANT
1. What are the expected student outcomes of the science curriculum?	1. We need to have goals and to be clear about our vision for student development in science.
2. How well are students performing on the expected outcomes?	2. We need to know how well we are meeting our goals. Are we progressing in such a way that it is likely that we will meet our ultimate student outcomes?
3. What topics are covered by grade level, and how much time is spent on each?	3. We need to know what we are doing to meet our goals.
4. What methods and materials are used for each topic, and how good are they?	4. We need to analyze our instruction to identify targets for improvement.
5. To what extent is the curriculum meeting our expectations?	5. We need to be clear about our standards and the extent to which we are meeting them.

"All right, let's add it. Anything else?" With no other questions appearing, the committee members then narrowed down the list to a manageable set of questions. They started by examining why each question was important. When they could not come up with a good rationale for asking the question, they checked with the person who had asked it originally. If that person really did not think the question was important, they dropped it; the last thing they needed was to address questions that no one had an interest in. They eliminated four questions right off.

The members then looked for questions that were impossible to answer given the committee's time frame, resources, and evaluation technology. One parent had asked what other schools around the country were doing in science. The committee members agreed that if they could not find a national study already done, they would not undertake one themselves. They agreed, however, that they might call a few of the best school districts in the state and ask them to share their elementary curriculum. Similarly, a school board member had asked what students who had graduated from Lakeview City Central High School were doing in science. The members agreed that although the question was important, it went beyond their charge and capability of answering.

The remaining list was still too long to address this year by this committee. Mr. Henry said, "All right. We still need to narrow down our study to the most critical questions and something that is manageable. Let's look at each question and ask ourselves who is going to be angry if we don't address it. If the answer is no one, let's file it for some future time. Also, if anyone is aware of an already-existing answer to a question, speak up and we'll report it as part of our study. Maybe we can get credit for something that is already done. Why not?"

The committee struggled but finally agreed on the five questions listed in Figure 2.3 as the most critical ones to address. The rationales for asking each question are listed in the second column of the table. Mr. Henry agreed to share the list with Mrs. Goss and with all other teachers in the school with a note saying that these would be the questions the science evaluation study would address. Anyone who had a comment or reaction to the list was invited to meet with the committee to discuss revising the list. Otherwise, the committee would go with the list as it was. When the list and note were distributed, no one suggested changing the list of questions.

The next chapter will discuss collecting the information needed to answer evaluation questions.

3

COLLECTING
INFORMATION

To complete columns 3 and 4 in the evaluation worksheet (see Figure 2.2), you will have to identify the information you need to answer each question and then specify when and how the information will be collected. These two columns provide a structure for the methods that will be used to conduct the evaluation.

INFORMATION NEEDS AND SOURCES

For each question in the first column of the worksheet, one must ask what information is needed to answer the question. Usually, the response is fairly straightforward. For example, if the question is, "How well are students performing on science objectives?" the information needed to answer the question might be scores on teacher-made unit tests, results on a state assessment test, or standardized achievement test results. But the answer might also include results on a career-interest inventory; an "attitudes toward science" questionnaire; and performance assessments in which, for example, students might have a chance to solve problems or make decisions while working on a science project.

Where to get the information is also an important consideration. You should use data already in existence whenever possible. This will save a lot of time and money, which are usually in short supply in schools. If the information is not readily available, then you need to think about who or where the best information source will be. Here is a list of common sources of information in school program evaluation:

- Students
- Teachers
- Principals or program directors
- School board members
- State education department staff
- Parents
- University specialists
- Direct observation of the program
- Libraries and public documents (reports, textbooks, research studies, dissertations)
- School files and records
- Professional associations

If the source of critical information is not evident, it is permissible and simple enough to ask others for suggestions about where you might best obtain such information. This is also a good way to involve stakeholders in the evaluation. Also, keep in mind that you can only do what is feasible. In many cases of in-house evaluation, informal discussions and other less formal methods might be appropriate.

IDENTIFYING METHODS AND INSTRUMENTS FOR COLLECTING INFORMATION

The methods that evaluators use to collect information change with every evaluation. There often is no single method or instrument that can satisfy the information needs of all questions that might be asked. Consequently, evaluators must carry with them a toolbox of alternative methods and instruments to draw from as the need arises. What follows is a listing of common formal methods and instruments used to gather information in program evaluation. A book could be written about how to develop and use each method (and such books have been written), but a detailed or technical discussion goes beyond what is possible in this guide and is not the intent here. This section of the guide provides a list of alternative ways that may be used to collect information. The details are left up to the many excellent and already-existing references that are cited. With each method is a reference list of one or more other sources in case more detail is needed about any particular method or instrument.

Often, informal methods of data collection such as group discussions, informal observations, and reflections of key informants will also be appropriate for school program evaluations. Do not overlook any sources of information when you are conducting an evaluation. You want the best evidence available to guide you when you are making decisions.

Surveys are collections of questions on a small number of issues given to a large number of potential respondents. Surveys can be done through the mail (using questionnaires), over the telephone (using interviewers), in person (e.g., in a house-to-house survey using interviewers), or with intact groups (e.g., with a form that is distributed at a meeting or in a classroom). Follow-ups should be used with nonrespondents in mail surveys and with those not found to be at home in telephone or household interview surveys. Surveys are a commonly used method for data collection in program evaluation. **SURVEYS**

For more details about how to conduct surveys, you should find the following sources helpful:

> Dillman, D. A. (1978). *Mail and telephone surveys: The total design method.* New York: John Wiley.
> Fink, A., & Kosecoff, J. (1998). *How to conduct surveys* (2nd ed.). Thousand Oaks, CA: Sage.
> Gall, M. D., Borg, W. R., & Gall, J. P. (1996). *Educational research* (6th ed.). New York: Longman.

Testing is by far the most common method of collecting information from and about students in education. In testing for student achievement, there are two major categories of tests: (a) norm-referenced tests, and (b) criterion-referenced tests. **TESTING**

Norm-Referenced Testing

Norm-referenced tests compare a student's performance on a broad range of skills and knowledge against those of other students who took the same test. The administration procedures are standardized. Examples include the Iowa Tests of Basic Skills, the Iowa Tests of Educational Development, the Stanford Achievement Test, the Metropolitan Achievement Test, the California Achievement Test, and the Comprehensive Test of Basic Skills.

Criterion-Referenced Testing

Criterion-referenced tests assess a student's performance on a domain of skills or on a set of instructional objectives or standards. Examples include textbook unit tests, teacher-made tests, basic skills competency tests, and performance tests. Criterion-referenced tests are used most commonly in internal program evaluations by school personnel. In recent years, schools have begun assembling portfolios of different kinds of evidence of what a student can do. By using a wide range of student assessments, educators believe they can get a better picture of a student's abilities and achievements than they can by using one multiple-choice, paper-and- pencil test.

Standards governing the use of tests are available and are must reading for anyone using tests with students. These standards include *Standards for Teacher Competence in Educational Assessment of Students, Code of Fair Testing Practices in Education, Code of Professional Responsibilities in Educational Measurement,* and *Standards for Educational and Psychological Testing.* Information about obtaining copies of these documents is available from the National Council on Measurement in Education, 1230 17th Street NW, Washington, DC 20036, or from the ERIC Clearinghouse on Assessment and Evaluation, http://ericae.net.

GUIDELINES FOR TESTING

If you are going to develop a test, some guidelines for writing good tests include the following:

- Be sure to be clear about what it is you want to measure.
- Develop a blueprint for the test that lists the topics to be covered in your content domain and the category of your objectives in Bloom's taxonomy (Bloom, Englehart, Furst, Hill, & Krathwohl, 1956; see also Resource B).
- Select the item formats to fit the kind of behavior you want demonstrated by your students:
  —Essay tests for organizing thoughts, writing skills, and synthesis of knowledge
  —True-false and multiple-choice items for covering a wide range of topics; ease and objectivity in scoring; and also recognition, recall, and application responses
  —Short-answer and completion items for recall of knowledge, covering a wide range of topics, and relative ease and objectivity in scoring
  —Matching items for recognition of correct responses, ease and objectivity in scoring, and covering a wide range of topics examining relationships
- Use clear directions.
- Allow enough time for completion.
- Keep the reading difficulty of the test items appropriate to what is being measured.
- Be careful that one test item does not give a clue for answering another.
- Avoid ambiguity.
- Avoid trivia.

- Beware of "specific determiners" such as *never* and *always*.
- Beware of giving cues to the correct answer through the length of the response choice.
- Be sure there is only one correct or clearly best answer.
- Develop more items than you need, pilot-test them, and select the best.

Examples of essay, true-false, multiple-choice, short-answer and completion, and matching test items are shown below.

Sample Essay Test Items

1. Surveys and tests are common methods for collecting information in program evaluation. Distinguish between the two methods by indicating how they are the same and how they are different. Indicate when you would use each.

   _____

   _____

   _____

2. Identify two sources of information that you would use to help design a survey study and two sources of information that you would use to help develop a test. Give a summary of the information each source will provide.

   _____

   _____

   _____

3. Attached is a report of a survey study. Read the report and then indicate whether the study is good or bad. Give your reasons for your judgment and cite specific parts of the study to support your reasons.

   _____

   _____

   _____

Sample True-False Test Items

1. A "blueprint" for a test lists the format for the items to be included on the test.

   True   False

2. True-false items are used to assess writing skills.
     True   False

3. True-false test items can cover a relatively wide range of topics in a short span of time.
     True   False

Sample Multiple-Choice Test Items

1. In program evaluation, information collection follows
   a. Focusing the evaluation
   b. Analyzing information
   c. Reporting information
   d. Evaluating the evaluation
2. Follow-ups are conducted in surveys when
   a. The response rate is 100%
   b. There is a large number of nonrespondents
   c. A question was left off the questionnaire
   d. The questionnaires are lost
3. An example of a criterion-reference test is
   a. The Stanford Achievement Test
   b. The Iowa Test of Basic Skills
   c. The Metropolitan Achievement Test
   d. A teacher-made test

Sample Short-Answer and Completion Test Items

1. Two test item formats that are used to collect information about student recall of knowledge are _____ and _____.

2. Define norm-referenced testing: (short answer)

   _____

   _____

3. When are surveys used for information collections? (short answer)

   _____

   _____

Sample Matching Test Items

For each test item format in the list at the left, select the *best* use of that format from the list at the right.

_____ 1. Essay   a. Assess ability to synthesize
_____ 2. True-false   b. Assess recall of definitions
_____ 3. Short answer   c. Assess recognition of relationships
_____ 4. Matching   d. Assess the most content in a limited
                                   amount of time

Notice how the reading difficulty in each of these examples is kept as simple as possible. The examples are clear and to the point, covering important topics. The multiple-choice items avoid the use of *never, always, all of the above*, and *none of the above*. Finally, each item has one best answer.

Your school district could benefit from starting a test or item file for each school subject. You could start by collecting tests and test items used by your teachers and then asking neighboring districts to share theirs. Eventually, you could build your collection by soliciting tests and items from all school districts in the state.

For more details about testing, you should find the following sources helpful:

Airasian, P. W. (1997). *Classroom assessment.* New York: McGraw-Hill.
Hopkins, K. D. (1998). *Educational and psychological measurement in evaluation* (8th ed.). Boston: Allyn & Bacon.

In addition, commercially available tests are listed in *Tests in Print* and reviewed in the *Mental Measurements Yearbooks* published by the Buros Institute at the University of Nebraska. Test collections are available from the Educational Testing Service, Princeton, NJ, http://www.ets.org.

QUESTIONNAIRES

Questionnaires are collections of standard questions about a few issues placed on a form for response. Most questionnaires are developed locally, because the issues are idiosyncratic. When developing a questionnaire, it is always wise to pilot-test it by asking available people to attempt to complete it. They can usually tell you about confusing directions and unclear questions.

GUIDELINES FOR QUESTIONNAIRES

Some guidelines for developing a questionnaire include the following:

- Provide clear instructions, including a due date.
- Do not ask leading questions.
- Group questions according to topic.
- Make it attractive.
- Keep it short.
- Do not assume too much knowledge.
- Begin by asking easy, impersonal questions.
- Do not ask double questions (i.e., two questions in one).
- State questions precisely.

An example of a questionnaire follows.

Sample Questionnaire

Please answer each of the following questions according to your best judgment or knowledge. There are no right or wrong answers, and your name will not be associated with your responses. All responses will be aggregated and reported for the total faculty. Please return this questionnaire by May 1.

1. In general, how would you rate the science resource room as a facility for providing necessary science instruction to your students?
   ____ Excellent, no problems
   ____ Good, a few problems
   ____ Average, several problems
   ____ Poor, many problems
   ____ Awful, filled with problems

2. How often do you use the science resource room per month on average?
   ____ Not at all
   ____ 1-2 times
   ____ 3-4 times
   ____ 5-6 times
   ____ 7-8 times
   ____ More than 8 times

3. a. Are the facilities of the science resource room adequate?
        Yes   No

   b. If no, what is needed?

4. a. Do you have problems getting access to the science resource room?
        Yes   No

   b. If yes, please describe the problem?

5. a. Was your orientation to the science resource room adequate?
        Yes   No

   b. If no, what is needed?

6. What can be done to improve the science resource room?

Notice how the questions are kept short and to the point. The instructions are clear and questions are stated precisely. No double questions are asked, and questions are worded so that they do not lead the respondent to answer in a certain way.

For more details about developing questionnaires, you should find the following sources useful:

Dillman, D. A. (1978). *Mail and telephone surveys: The total design method.* New York: John Wiley.

Fink, A. (1995). *The Survey Kit.* Thousand Oaks, CA: Sage.

Fowler, F. J., Jr. (1989). *Survey research methods* (2nd ed.). Newbury Park, CA: Sage.

Gall, M. D., Borg, W. R., & Gall, J. P. (1996). *Educational research* (6th ed.). New York: Longman.

Interviews are used to deliver questions and record responses when a personal contact is needed to boost the rate of response, to probe beyond initial responses, or to get a fast response. Interviewers need to be trained because their personal behaviors and appearance can affect the responses they receive. They are a critical part of the interview process. — INTERVIEWS

Some guidelines for an interview schedule (the questionnaire used by interviewers) include the following: — GUIDELINES FOR INTERVIEWS

- Keep the language pitched to the level of the respondent.
- Establish rapport by asking easy, impersonal questions first.
- Avoid long questions.
- Avoid ambiguous wording.
- Avoid leading questions.
- Limit questions to a single idea.
- Do not assume too much knowledge.

An example of an interview schedule follows.

Sample Interview Schedule

The questions I am about to ask you concern our science resource materials. Please be frank when responding. Your name will not be associated with your responses. We will compile all faculty responses into an aggregated report.

1. First, we want to know how you are using the materials. In what ways are you using them?

   Probe questions:

   a. What ways of using these materials have you found especially satisfactory? Why do you think these ways have been so satisfactory?

   b. Have you tried some things you won't try again? What are they? Why wouldn't you use them again?
   c. Which materials have you used? Why did you select these materials?
2. Next, we want to learn whether the use of the science materials has made any difference in your students' achievements. Has the use of the science materials resulted in student achievement?
   Probe questions:
   a. What difference has it made? Which materials made a difference?
   b. Do the materials cause you to spend more time on certain topics? Which topics?
   c. Do all students benefit? Which ones do or do not? Why?

Notice that the questions are clear and worded in an easy style. Each set of questions covers a single topic. The questions are not leading but do probe into details about the response given by the interviewee.

For more details about developing questionnaires, you should find the following sources helpful:

Dillman, D. A. (1978). *Mail and telephone surveys: The total design method.* New York: John Wiley.
Fowler, F. J., Jr. (1989). *Survey research methods* (2nd ed.). Newbury Park, CA: Sage.
Fowler, F. J., Jr., & Mangione, T. W. (1990). *Standardized survey interviewing: Minimizing interviewer-related error.* Newbury Park, CA: Sage.
Gall, M. D., Borg, W. R., & Gall, J. P. (1996). *Educational research* (6th ed.). New York: Longman.
Gordon, R. L. (1980). *Interviewing: Strategy, techniques, and tactics.* Homewood, IL: Dorsey.

ATTITUDE SCALES
Attitudes are predispositions toward some group, institution, or abstract concept. This is one method for collecting information where it is advised that you select from existing instruments, such as collections of attitude scales, rather than constructing your own. Fortunately, there are many such instruments available. If the available scales do not hit your target exactly, you can modify the wording of the scales, keeping the format intact, without causing too much damage to the original purpose of the instrument.

An example of a Likert-type attitude scale follows.

Sample Attitude Scale

SA = *Strongly Agree*
A = *Agree*
U = *Undecided*
D = *Disagree*
SD = *Strongly Disagree*

Circle the response that best fits your feelings. There are no right or wrong answers. Your name will not be associated with your response.

1. Science is my favorite subject.	SA	A	U	D	SD
2. I feel especially capable when studying science.	SA	A	U	D	SD
3. It is easy to get good marks in science.	SA	A	U	D	SD
4. Science exercises often scare me.	SA	A	U	D	SD
5. Science requires too much of my time.	SA	A	U	D	SD
6. Science is very useful in life.	SA	A	U	D	SD
7. What we are asked to do in science is just too much.	SA	A	U	D	SD
8. Science often makes my mind go blank.	SA	A	U	D	SD
9. More school time should be given to science.	SA	A	U	D	SD
10. I enjoy reading science books in my spare time.	SA	A	U	D	SD

Notice that each statement addresses some aspect of feelings about the topic, science. The statements are clearly worded, short, and to the point. The statements are a mixture of positive and negative attitudes. The directions provide guidance in how to respond.

Sources of attitude scales include the following:

Robinson, J. P., Shaver, P. R., & Wrightsman, L. S. (Eds.). (1991). *Measures of personality and social psychological attitudes.* New York: Academic Press.
Shaw, M. R., & Wright, J. M. (1967). *Scales for measurement of attitudes.* New York: McGraw-Hill.

Commercially available attitude instruments may also be found in *Tests in Print* and the *Mental Measurements Yearbooks* published by the Buros Institute at the University of Nebraska. Attitude scales may also be found in the ETS test collection, available through the ERIC Clearinghouse on Assessment and Evaluation, http://www.ericae.net.

OBSERVATION CHECKLISTS

Observation checklists can be selected from existing instruments, or they can be developed locally. Fortunately, there is a very useful collection of classroom observation process instruments, edited by A. Simon and E. G. Boyer (1974), called *Mirrors of Behavior: An Anthology of Observation Instruments* (Philadelphia: Research for Better Schools). If you are going to take an inventory of whether certain conditions exist in your school or classroom, you can simply compile the list of desirable characteristics and then check off those that do exist.

An example of an observation checklist follows.

Sample Observation Checklist

Check those items that you see in evidence in the classroom you visit.
_____ Aquarium
_____ Science-related bulletin board
_____ Science posters on the wall
_____ Science resource books
_____ Science laboratory equipment
_____ A/V materials on science
_____ Live animals
_____ Bird feeder
_____ Scientific measurement instruments
_____ Other science-related materials (please list)

Notice that the checklist provides a clear set of directions about how to respond. All items on the checklist are things that are clearly observable and evidence of science activity in the classroom. The checklist should be as comprehensive (i.e., exhaustive of indicators of science activities) as possible.

UNOBTRUSIVE MEASURES

Unobtrusive measures are methods for collecting information without affecting the natural behaviors of those who are being studied. You simply gather evidence without anyone being aware that it is happening. Consequently, unobtrusive (or nonreactive) measures often capture human behavior in its natural or typical form rather than in a contrived or peak-performance form. Another way of looking at unobtrusive measures is that you need to get creative when other forms of collecting information will not work or are not feasible. You need to ask yourself, "How will I know if I see it?" (referring to the behavior you want to measure) and then find ways to collect appropriate information. Unobtrusive measures can be informal observations, worn carpets in a certain location, worn books, actual use (consumption) of materials, archival records (e.g., library checkouts), newspaper or other mass media archival files, minutes, listening to informal conversations (and taking notes), absences, assignments, projects, grades, performances, and noting physical locations of people or objects. Basically, unobtrusive measures consist of *physical traces, archives,* and *observations.*

Metfessel and Michael (1967) have developed a useful listing of multiple ways to measure the things we are interested in assessing in school programs. The classic source on unobtrusive measures is

Webb, E. J., Campbell, D. T., Schwartz, R. D., & Sechrest, L. (1966). *Unobtrusive measures: Nonreactive research in the social sciences.* Chicago: Rand McNally.

Document analysis is used to summarize the content of a document or even a series of similar documents (so that trends can be noted over time). For example, by analyzing minutes of meetings or newspaper coverage on a topic of interest, the evaluator may find both the number of times a topic was covered and whether the discussion was positive or negative, as well as what changes were being discussed or recommended. This is a good way to get a sense of community feeling concerning a program, especially if it is a controversial one.

DOCUMENT ANALYSIS

For more details on content analysis, you should find the following sources helpful:

Budd, R. W., Thop, R. K., & Donohew, L. (1967). *Content analysis of communication.* New York: Macmillan.

Denzin, N. K., & Lincoln, Y. S. (Eds.). (1994). *Handbook of qualitative research.* Thousand Oaks, CA: Sage.

Guba, E. G., & Lincoln, Y. S. (1981). *Effective evaluation.* San Francisco: Jossey-Bass.

Holsti, O. (1969). *Content analysis for the social sciences and humanities.* Reading, MA: Addison-Wesley.

The formal methods and instruments listed above are commonly used in program evaluations. It would be a good idea to begin building a professional library at your school that includes the reference sources cited with each method or type of instrument and also to include existing instruments that you can keep on file and modify as needed for a particular program evaluation. Please keep in mind, however, that informal ways of gathering information are perfectly acceptable when formal data collection is simply not feasible.

VALIDITY AND RELIABILITY

Two concepts to keep in mind when selecting a method or instrument for collecting information are *validity* and *reliability.* Validity is concerned with whether the instrument or method hits the target in providing you with the information you need. For example, many commercially available tests or "off-the-shelf" instruments would not cover the topics and objectives of Johnson Elementary School's science program. They lack validity for that purpose. In *Statistics: A Spectator Sport* (1990), Richard Jaeger points out,

VALIDITY

When we collect data on a person for the purpose of research in education or the social sciences, we usually measure or observe a *sample* of that person's behavior. We might provide the person with a task to be completed or some set of stimulus materials that require a response. A traditional pencil-and-paper test is a good example. Alternatively, we might just observe the person in some naturally occurring situation, and count the incidences of some behavior or action. In recent years, much educational research has included observations of the incidence of specified students' or teachers' behaviors in classrooms. For example, a researcher might count the number of times, in a 15-minute period, that a teacher asks his or her students a direct question.

If research merely involved reporting the number of test items a person answered correctly, or the number of times a teacher asked his or her students a question, there would be few validity issues. Validity concerns arise because researchers interpret these observable behaviors as indicators of a person's status on more general constructs such as "ability" or "interest." By generalizing beyond observed behaviors that occur at a particular time and in a particular setting, researchers and evaluators create a multitude of validity issues. The most fundamental concern is the appropriateness of the interpretations of the results of measurement. Measurement procedures are not *inherently* valid, nor inherently invalid. It is the *interpretations* of measurement results that must be examined for validity. (pp. 79-80)

There are four types of evidence that are frequently used to indicate measurement validity. As Jaeger (1990) tells us, they are

- *Construct validity,* which is concerned with the total relationship between the results of a particular measurement and the underlying construct the evaluator is attempting to measure.
- *Concurrent validity,* which is the correlation between an accepted measure of some construct and a new, yet unvalidated measure when they are taken at approximately the same time.
- *Predictive validity,* which is the correlation between a measure used to predict some future performance and the measure used to indicate future performance.
- *Content validity,* which is the degree to which the content of an instrument is representative of a larger domain of tasks or questions to which we want to generalize. There is no statistical evidence of content validity; it involves judging the content of an instrument. Often, evaluators will use a blueprint or table of specifications to show how many questions on an instrument are used to measure each issue or type of behavior they want to assess.

RELIABILITY   Reliability is concerned with error of measurement and whether the instrument or method is giving you a stable reading. On the topic of reliability, Jaeger (1990) writes,

It is well known that no measurement procedure—whether it is the use of a bathroom scale or the administration of an achievement test—is perfectly consistent. If you were to step on and off your bathroom scale five times in a row, chances are you would observe three or four different measurements of your weight. Depending on whether you placed your feet in exactly the same spot on the scale, and on the quality of the scale itself, the scale's indication of your weight might fluctuate by three or four pounds across the five measurements. The more consistent the indications of your weight, the more reliable is your bathroom scale. If the scale were to indicate exactly the same weight for you every time you stepped on and off (a highly unlikely occurrence), it would be totally consistent. We would then say that it was perfectly "reliable" *even though it might indicate the wrong weight every time* and thus give you an invalid weight. (In the *everyday* sense of "reliable" we would include validity, too; but in the technical sense, validity is a completely separate issue.)

When you observe the weight indicated by your bathroom scale, you are reading what measurement theorists call an *observed score*. This observed score can be thought of as consisting of two parts: one is your true weight (the *true score*), and the other is the results of a variety of factors that have nothing to do with your true weight (the *error component*). These other factors might include such things as the particular position of your feet on the scale (step too far forward, and the scale might read low; step too far backward and it might read high); the fact that you placed the scale on a thick rug instead of on the floor; and the tendency of the scale's springs to fatigue and recover depending on the rates at which you climb on and off the scale. In every measurement procedure, regardless of what is being measured or how it is being measured, the observed score that results from taking a measurement is equal to the sum of the true score and the error component. The reliability of the measurement procedure depends on the relative sizes of the true score and the error component. The larger the error component, the lower the reliability; the smaller the error component, the higher the reliability.

Measurement reliability is usually expressed as an index that can take on values between 0 and 1, much like a correlation coefficient. Unlike a correlation coefficient, though, the reliability of a measurement procedure can never be a negative number. A reliability of 0 means that the observed scores consist entirely of error components. A reliability of 1 would mean that the observed scores consist entirely of true scores; in reality, however, observed scores are composed of both true scores and error components, and their reliabilities are less than 1. (pp. 85-86)

Many available instruments have reliability coefficients reported with them. Several methods can be used to assess reliability when it is unknown. One method, called the *test-retest* method, involves giving an instrument to the same group of people twice and then calculating the correlation between the two sets of scores. Reliability estimation methods that require an instrument to be administered only once are called *internal consistency* methods. They indicate to what degree all of the measurements used in a procedure assess the same construct. Split-half, odd-even, Kuder-Richardson, and Cronbach's alpha are all different approaches to internal consistency reliability estimation.

Reliability is a concern as well when informal data collection methods are used. For example, informal conversations, a form of unobtrusive measurement, can change in tone from one day to the next. In cases when you are using unobtrusive measures or other informal methods with suspect reliability, you should back up your information by going to several sources (e.g., documents in the files or survey results) to confirm what your unobtrusive measurements are telling you. This is called *triangulating,* because you are usually basing your decisions on three or more different sources, rather than just one. Professional news reporters often use this strategy as a means of achieving accurate reporting.

WHO WILL COLLECT
INFORMATION AND WHEN

The final piece of planning to go into the collection of information is deciding who will collect the information and when they will do it. Normally, the job of collecting information will fall on the group that is doing the evaluation. There are many times, however, when the evaluators must ask others to help administer a test or a questionnaire. Therefore, it is important to plan ahead to specify who will collect the information, under what conditions, and when. This information can be recorded in the fourth column of the worksheet as shown in Figure 3.1. A time schedule can then be made up for collecting data to answer each evaluation question; it will be important to talk to each person who will be participating to get everyone's cooperation and support. A follow-up memo to confirm dates and responsibilities can then be sent.

TIMING   The timing of information collection is an important consideration. First, keep in mind when the evaluation is to be completed and then work backward. Second, consider when the information is going to be available. When is the most appropriate time to be collecting this information? Finally, consider when the information can be conveniently collected. Certain times of the year—the beginning and ending of the school year, summers, holidays, exam periods—are not good times to be collecting information in schools. Consider class times, lunch times, recesses, special events, and teacher preferences in developing the schedules. Being educators, the evaluators have to be sensitive to the needs of others in the school.

When collecting information, keep in mind certain issues that will need to be addressed. These are very practical points that can greatly affect the quality of the evaluation.

Figure 3.1. Evaluation Information Collection and Analysis Worksheet (First Four Columns Completed)

Evaluation Questions	Why the Question Is Important	Information Needed to Answer the Question	When and How the Information Will Be Collected
1. What are the expected student outcomes of the science curriculum?	1. We need to have goals and to be clear about our vision for student development in science.	1. What each teacher of science expects; what our curriculum guides say.	1. In October, each teacher of science will be asked to list the 10 most important outcomes for students in science this year.
2. How well are students performing on the expected outcomes?	2. We need to know how well we are meeting our goals. Are we progressing in such a way that we will meet our ultimate student outcomes?	2. Achievement of students in science.	2. In May, each science teacher will be asked to list strong and weak outcomes of their students. In March, standardized science achievement scores and state assessment science scores will be compiled.
3. What topics are covered by grade level, and how much time is spent on each?	3. We need to know what we are doing to meet our goals.	3. What each teacher covers; what our curriculum guides say.	3. In January, each science teacher will be asked to list topics and time allocations for each for this year.
4. What methods and materials are used for each topic, and how good are they?	4. We need to analyze our instruction to identify targets for improvement.	4. What each teacher uses; teachers' judgments of strengths and weaknesses of methods and materials.	4. In January, each science teacher will also be asked to list methods and materials for each topic and to evaluate each.
5. To what extent is the curriculum meeting our expectations?	5. We need to be clear about our standards and the extent to which we are meeting them.	5. What others (e.g., NSTA, AAAS, state department of education, our curriculum guides) say about standards.	5. In November, curriculum standards from different sources will be compiled.

PRACTICAL
POINTERS FOR
COLLECTING
INFORMATION

1. *What do you do when you run into problems of noncooperation or people not taking the data collection seriously?* To avoid such problems, you should explain the evaluation and its importance fully to participants and obtain their support prior to the beginning of the evaluation. If problems occur during the evaluation, a private talk may help if you can show it is in everyone's best interest to participate. Sometimes, the use of confidentiality with questionnaires or interviews will alleviate concerns. Some form of payback (e.g., released time) may also work. It is important, however, to be on the lookout for potential problems and to deal with them immediately when they appear.

2. *What can go wrong in data collection?* Let us consider some of the possibilities (with possible solutions in parentheses):

    a. Respondents misunderstand directions and consequently respond inappropriately (pilot-test your methods).

    b. Inexperienced data collectors mess up (train your data collectors and conduct trial runs).

    c. Information gets lost (establish a rule that no original data leave the office; duplicate data and computer files; keep original data under lock and key).

    d. Information is recorded incorrectly (build in cross-checks of recorded information).

3. *When collecting information, take time to explain your purposes so that participants are informed about how the results might affect them.* This will help build rapport.

4. *Choose a pleasant environment for data collection if the session is going to take a while.* Good lighting and ventilation, comfortable seating, adequate spacing for group testing, and adequate monitoring for group testing are all recommended.

5. *Follow up with a thank you to any participants who went out of their way to provide information or to assist in the evaluation.*

Your plan is now taking shape.

To review, the collection of information involves the following:

1. Identifying sources of information for each evaluation question
2. Selecting evaluation methods that are appropriate for the evaluation questions being asked
3. Scheduling the collection of information
4. Assigning the tasks of collecting information to evaluation staff

Illustrative Case Study (Part 3)

The steering committee for the science program evaluation at Johnson Elementary School met for its regular Monday afternoon planning meeting to formulate plans for addressing the questions it had selected for the evaluation.

Mr. Henry began the meeting. "OK, it's time now to develop our plan for addressing the five questions and scheduling our work for the year. Let's begin. First, let's take each question and think about where we should go to get an accurate answer to the question. If we can go to several different sources, let's consider the easiest, most accessible source as the one we'll use. If we have some doubts about the accuracy of the information we'll get, we can go to two or three sources to make us feel better about the information we'll be basing our conclusions on. Let's start with question one."

After considerable discussion on each question, the committee arrived at the plans recorded in Figure 3.1. Recognizing that some teachers did not teach anything related to science, the committee decided that only those teachers who did teach science topics would be asked to participate. The members agreed to split up the task of going to those teachers and sharing the plan with them, asking for reactions and agreement to participate as planned. Each committee member took responsibility for contacting the other teachers at one grade level in Johnson Elementary. At a subsequent meeting, they were pleased to find out that they would get full cooperation.

The science steering committee also worked on the specifics of collecting information. Who was going to collect what, and when? Mr. Sanders stated, "If you think I'm going to do all of this, you're crazy. I've got enough to do being a good teacher. Besides, I've got a family, and I need to spend time with them!"

"I anticipated this problem," said Mr. Henry. "You are absolutely right that none of us has time to do what is necessary to carry this off. I talked to Mrs. Goss about this issue, and she agreed to cover my class as needed to release me to coordinate the evaluation. I will carry the ball, keep you informed, and then involve you at critical points, primarily in writing our report." There was a great sigh of relief in unison from five teachers. Mr. Henry smiled. "Now, let's work on specifics."

The work plan that the committee developed is presented in Table 3.1. Mr. Henry took this plan to Mrs. Goss and got her approval, and then he distributed it to the other teachers in the school with a cover memo explaining his role as evaluation coordinator. Everyone was fully informed and ready to participate.

You are now ready to prepare a plan for organizing and analyzing program evaluation.

TABLE 3.1   Evaluation Work Plan

Evaluation Questions	Tasks	Task Beginning and Ending Date	Personnel Involved	Other Resources Needed	Total Task Costs
1. What are the expected student outcomes of the science curriculum?	a. Create teacher survey form	a. September 1-30	a. Evaluation coordinator	a. Typist	$150 (duplication costs)
	b. Survey teachers	b. October 1-31	b. Evaluation coordinator	b. Duplication of forms	
	c. Compile results	c. November 1-30	c. Evaluation coordinator	c. None	
	d. Distribute to teachers for comment	d. December 1-15	d. Evaluation coordinator	d. Duplication of results; typist	
	e. Compare to curriculum	e. January 15-31	e. Science committee and evaluation coordinator	e. None	
	f. Review of findings by science committee	f. June 1-30	f. Science committee	f. Duplication of results	
	g. Prepare report of strengths and weaknesses by science committee	g. June 1-30	g. Science committee and evaluation coordinator	g. Typist; duplication of reports	
2. How well are students performing on the expected outcomes?	a. Create teacher survey form	a. April 1-30	a. Evaluation coordinator	a. Typist	$150 (duplication costs)
	b. Survey teachers	b. May 1-30	b. Evaluation coordinator	b. Duplication of forms	
	c. Compile survey results	c. June 1-15	c. Evaluation coordinator	c. None	
	d. Compile test results	d. March 1-30	d. Evaluation coordinator	d. None	
	e. Review of findings by science committee	e. June 15-30	e. Science committee	e. Duplication of results; typist	
	f. Prepare report of strengths and weaknesses by science committee	f. June 15-30	f. Science committee and evaluation coordinator	f. Typist; duplication of report	

Question	Task	Date	Responsible	Resources	Cost
3. What topics are covered by grade level, and how much time is spent on each?	a. Create teacher survey form	a. December 1-15	a. Evaluation coordinator	a. Typist	$150 (duplication costs)
	b. Survey teachers	b. January 15-31	b. Evaluation coordinator	b. Duplication of forms	
4. What methods and materials are used for each topic, and how good are they?	a. Compile survey results	a. February 1-28	a. Evaluation coordinator	a. None	
	b. Review of findings by science committee	b. June 1-30	b. Science committee	b. Typist; duplication of committee findings	
	c. Prepare report of strengths and weaknesses by science committee	c. June 15-30	c. Science committee and evaluation coordinator	c. Typist; duplication of committee findings	
5. To what extent is the curriculum meeting our expectations?	a. Compile standards for science curriculum from multiple sources	a. November 1-December 15	a. Evaluation coordinator	a. Cost of materials; postage; duplication	
	b. Analyze science curriculum against standards	b. January 1-February 28	b. Evaluation coordinator	b. None	
	c. Summarize strengths and weaknesses for science committee	c. January 1-February 28	c. Evaluation coordinator	c. Typist; duplication of findings	
	d. Review of findings and final report by science committee	d. June 1-30	d. Science committee and evaluation coordinator	d. Typist; duplication of findings	

4

ORGANIZING AND ANALYZING INFORMATION

For each evaluation question on the worksheet, you will now want to describe the way in which the information will be analyzed. This is important, because you can often be swamped with information. How can you summarize the information you collect so that the message from your data is accurate and clear? Several techniques will be considered in this section for analyzing qualitative (narrative) and quantitative (numerical) information and the means for conducting the analysis, such as using statistical software on a microcomputer, using a calculator, using a panel of readers from the staff of your school, or even hiring a consultant. If the consultant route is taken, it is best to involve the consultant in the very beginning of the evaluation planning. Do not wait until the information has been collected to seek outside help in analyzing it. The United States is full of overstocked data warehouses where unanalyzed information sits unused because of shortsightedness in the planning for data analysis. A little planning can save a lot of work at this point.

ORGANIZING AND ANALYZING QUALITATIVE INFORMATION

The best advice for organizing narrative information (e.g., field notes, transcripts of interviews, written responses to open-ended questions, and copies of documents) includes the following:

ANALYZING
QUALITATIVE
INFORMATION

1. Make sure it is all there.

2. Make copies for safe storage, for writing on, and for cutting and pasting.

3. Organize it as it comes in. Three hours of work organizing and summarizing for each hour of work collecting is a good rule of thumb. Some ways of filing information are by topic (e.g., school climate, teaching methods), by respondents (e.g., teacher data, student data), by event (e.g., the science fair), or by calendar (e.g., September data). Use a cut-up-and-put-in-folder or card-system approach to group common items. For example, all information about the effectiveness of a new teaching unit can be filed together. With today's modern computer software, you might even consider doing this by computer.

4. Take stock during data collection and at the end about what you are finding.

5. Use your human computer (your brain) to draw conclusions and then back them up with the information you have collected. That is, make the best case you can for your findings.

6. Verify and validate your findings by getting reactions from people who were there.

The best analyses of qualitative data use intellectual rigor and documentation to support conclusions.

ORGANIZING AND ANALYZING QUANTITATIVE INFORMATION

Sometimes, program evaluation information will be numerical data that will require some form of statistical analysis to create a meaningful and accurate summary. Consider the methods and instruments listed in Chapter 3 and the kinds of data each will generate. You can plan your quantitative data analyses by considering each method or instrument and how you will deal with the data it generates.

TESTING

Norm-referenced standardized testing companies typically will provide a clear, easily interpreted summary for your school, for each classroom, and for individual students if requested. In program evaluation, one usually is most interested in classroom and school statistics. The use of each of the following types of statistics is illustrated in the following pages in the context of data that may be collected in a program evaluation.

The *mean*, or average raw score, tells us how a typical student in the classroom or building performed. Because the mean will correspond to a fictional student, the score does not reflect the performance of any one individual. It does represent the performance level of the class or the school in the form of an "individual."

A *frequency distribution* tells us how many students scored at each score level in the classroom or the school. This gives us better information about how the class is doing than does the mean alone. Bar charts or other graphs can be used to report this information.

The *variance* or *standard deviation* tells us how spread out the students' scores are for a given classroom or school. The more spread out or heterogeneous the group is, the bigger the value of the variance or standard deviation will be. By comparing standard deviations across classrooms or schools, or by comparing them to standard deviations of zero, you can see how close together or spread apart the students in any one classroom, grade level, or school actually are. For example, if the standard deviation of this year's 10th-grade standardized achievement test raw scores in science is 4.80, and last year it was 12.50 for the 10th grade, we could conclude that this year the 10th graders were performing much more alike than 10th graders did last year. They are more homogeneous in science achievement this year.

The computational procedures for these techniques go beyond the purpose of this guide, but references to introductory statistics books are provided as an aid at the end of this section. Statistical software packages are available now for use on most personal microcomputers.

ANALYZING QUANTITATIVE TESTING INFORMATION

SURVEY QUESTIONNAIRE OR INTERVIEW

You usually will be most interested in the responses to each question on the questionnaire. Consequently, you should list each question and then summarize the responses for the question. For structured questions where respondents check one option out of several provided, you would do as follows:

1. (List the questions)	(frequency)	(percentage)
a. (list answer options)		
b.		
c.		
d.		

An example of reporting summary statistics for structured questionnaire items is shown below.

Do you plan to be involved in future science in-service activities?		
Yes	78	54.9%
Not sure	19	13.4%
No (retired)	1	0.7%
No response	44	31.0%

As indicated above, you should provide the frequency (tally) and percentage response for each option. The frequency distribution in this example shows that a majority (54.9%) of respondents plan to be involved in future science in-service activities. For some reason, there were a large number of people who did not respond to the question. One might want to contact those 44 people again to ask them why they did not respond.

For open-ended questions where respondents write a short response, you would again list the question and then provide the verbatim responses if there are a small number of respondents (e.g., less than 20). Then, give a verbal summary of the responses. If there are a large number of respondents, categories of responses should be formed, and then the frequencies and percentages of responses falling into each category should be reported.

Sometimes, you will be interested in seeing if there is a relationship between responses on one item and responses on another item on the survey form. An example of this is shown below.

| | *Do you plan to attend future science inservice activities?* | |
How many years have you been teaching?	*Yes*	*No/Not Sure*
0-5	48	0
6-10	20	0
11-15	9	10
Over 15	1	10

You may use a *correlation coefficient* to describe a relationship when responses are numbers (e.g., age, test score, or amount of time on task). It is obvious just from looking at this example that the younger teachers are most likely to attend future science in-service activities. This helps program coordinators target their presentations.

ATTITUDE SCALES

The formats for attitude scales differ across instruments, and it is hard to make general statements about the best approach to data analysis. One of the most common formats, however, is a *Likert scale,* in which a statement is given and the respondent is to respond on a 5-point scale labeled "strongly agree" on one end and "strongly disagree" on the other. In this case, each item can be analyzed as follows:

	Strongly Agree	*Agree*	*Not Sure*	*Disagree*	*Strongly Disagree*
1. (Statement)					
(frequency)					
(percentage)					
mean score =					
standard deviation =					

The frequency and percent of responses at each scale point can be recorded, and then the mean and standard deviation for the responses can be calculated. This would be done for each item. An example follows:

	Strongly Agree	Agree	Not Sure	Disagree	Strongly Disagree
1. The new science textbook teaches students how to solve problems on their own.	139	396	107	56	11
	19.6%	55.9%	15.1%	7.9%	1.6%

mean score = 3.84

standard deviation = 2.15

In this example, about 75% of the teachers agreed or strongly agreed that the new science textbook teaches problem solving. The mean, or average, is close to the "agree" point on the scale (3.84). The standard deviation (2.15) tells us there was not perfect agreement, that is, there was some spread in the responses.

If the Likert scale has been developed so that all statements are getting at the same issue in different ways, a total score can be calculated for each respondent, and then the total scores can be analyzed for a group of respondents as though they were test scores. In other words, a mean, standard deviation, and frequency distribution can be calculated to summarize the total group of scores.

OBSERVATION CHECKLISTS

Again, observation checklists vary greatly in format, and it is hard to provide a general procedure for data analysis that would hold for all cases. In many cases, frequency counts will suffice. Usually, however, the guide that accompanies a published observation checklist will provide procedures for data analysis. In most cases, procedures that have already been discussed will be used to summarize observations—means, standard deviations, and frequency distributions to describe group data. Correlation coefficients may be used to relate one observed behavior to another.

These are the techniques used most often in quantitative data analysis. For further information and computational procedures, see the following sources:

Hopkins, K. D., Hopkins, B. R., & Glass, G. V. (1996). *Basic statistics for the behavioral sciences* (3rd ed.). Boston: Allyn & Bacon.

Jaeger, R. M. (1990). *Statistics: A spectator sport* (2nd ed.). Newbury Park, CA: Sage.

Interpreting the Information

Once the information for the evaluation has been collected and analyzed, the job of evaluation is not done. In fact, in one sense it is just beginning, because the process of evaluation involves both description and judgment. The final step before reporting the results is to attach value judgments to the information now available. What does it mean for your program? What are the implications for program improvement? For change? These are questions that the evaluators should not answer alone; the major stakeholders should respond as well.

Numbers do not speak for themselves. Each member of your group will have a concept of what the data mean. This is to be expected, because of different experiences, training, roles in the program, expectations, and educational philosophies. Your group's members simply are not all the same person and would not all come up with the same set of recommendations after reviewing the information collected in the program evaluation.

Consequently, it is advised that you organize a stakeholder meeting. About 2 weeks before the meeting, information summaries should be sent to each meeting participant. The information should be organized by evaluation question so that all of the information pertaining to each question is displayed under that question. Participants should then be asked to read and digest all of this information about the program and to come to the meeting prepared to answer the following questions:

1. *What are the strengths and what are the weaknesses of this program?* Be able to support your statements with data.
2. *What are the implications of your analysis for changing the program?* That is, what are the areas that need improvement?

STAKEHOLDER
MEETINGS
At the meeting, each participant, including the evaluators, should be allowed to speak without interruption. A summary of the comments provided at the meeting should be part of the evaluation report. Where there are areas of common agreement, this fact should be noted. Where there are minority views, these, too, should be noted. This interpretation process will provide direction for program development in the coming years. It will also provide an important role in the evaluation for key stakeholders. Because of this, it is a critical step in the evaluation process.

Beyond the stakeholder meeting, you also have a responsibility to report how the program compares to known standards:

- Program goals
- Standards set by national organizations
- Standards set by model school districts or models based on professional literature (e.g., "what works," or "effective schools")

This chapter can be summarized by the following key points:

1. Select a method for analyzing qualitative and quantitative information that is appropriate for each evaluation question and the method used to collect the information.
2. Involve key stakeholders in interpreting the meaning and implications of the evaluation results.

Illustrative Case Study (Part 4)

Mr. Henry took the evaluation plan home with him and thought through how he would be analyzing the information collected during the year and how he would involve the science steering committee. He decided that the other committee members could play an important role in interpreting the results along with him. This process would reduce the pressure on him to have all the answers, which he knew he did not have. The data analysis and interpretation procedures that Mr. Henry inserted in the plan are found in the fifth column of the worksheet in Table 4.1.

This brings us to Chapter 5, which will discuss the reporting of information.

TABLE 4.1   Evaluation Information Collection and Analysis Worksheet (All Columns Completed)

Evaluation Questions	Why the Question Is Important	Information Needed to Answer the Question	When and How the Information Will Be Collected	Analysis and Interpretation
1. What are the expected student outcomes of the science curriculum?	1. We need to have goals.	1. What each teacher of science expects; what our curriculum guides say.	1. In October, each teacher of science will be asked to list the 10 most important outcomes for students in science this year.	1. A grade-by-grade listing of what teachers provided will be produced and distributed to teachers. These listings will be compared to curriculum guides and will be evaluated by the science committee.
2. How well are students performing on the expected outcomes?	2. We need to know how well we are meeting our goals.	2. Achievement of students in science.	2. In May, each science teacher will be asked to list strong and weak outcomes of their students. In March, standardized science achievement scores and state assessment science scores will be compiled.	2. A grade-by-grade listing of strengths and weaknesses of students in science will be prepared in June by the science committee.

Question	Rationale	Sources	Plan (January/November)	Plan (March/June)
3. What topics are covered by grade level, and how much time is spent on each?	3. We need to know what we are doing to meet our goals.	3. What each teacher covers; what our curriculum guides say.	3. In January, each science teacher will be asked to list topics and time allocations for each for this year.	3. & 4. A grade-by-grade listing of topics, times spent on each, methods, and materials will be prepared in March. This listing and teachers' judgments about needs in methods and materials will be evaluated by the science committee.
4. What methods and materials are used for each topic, and how good are they?	4. We need to analyze our instruction to identify targets for improvement.	4. What each teacher uses; teachers' judgments of strengths and weaknesses of methods and materials.	4. In January, each science teacher will also be asked to list methods and materials for each topic and to evaluate each.	
5. To what extent is the curriculum meeting our expectations?	5. We need to be clear about our standards and the extent to which we are meeting them.	5. What others (e.g., NSTA, AAAS, state department of education, our curriculum guides) say about standards.	5. In November, curriculum standards from different sources will be compiled.	5. The curriculum will be compared to known standards by the science committee in June. A final report of strengths and weaknesses will be prepared by the committee after reviewing all of the evaluation information collected during the year.

5

Reporting Information

Throughout the course of the evaluation, it is wise to keep participants and stakeholders informed about the evaluation process and the progress being made toward its completion. When preparing the final report of the evaluation, you need to keep in mind the purpose of the evaluation, the major audiences (decision makers) for the results, and the best medium to communicate with different audiences.

The evaluation will often have other teachers as the main audience. To overlook any of them would be a mistake. Typically, you will also want to share your recommendations with others, such as a member of the school board, the superintendent, your building principal, a parent group, or other participants in the evaluation. It will be important to consider what questions each wanted to have addressed and then to consider the best way to communicate with each audience. In some school studies, modest forms of reporting evaluation findings and recommendations, such as a memo, committee report, or program plan, may be most appropriate.

AUDIENCES

Once a draft report is completed, you should circulate the draft to key stakeholders for comments. This is an important step, because even the smallest factual errors can be used to discredit the evaluation. Evaluators are human, and it cannot be assumed that the report will be completely accurate and omniscient. Reviewers could be asked to comment on the following:

REVIEW OF DRAFT REPORT

- Factual errors
- Typing errors

- Plausible interpretations that are missing
- Additional evidence that might have been missed
- Any other suggestions that might improve the writing style or appearance of the report

Once comments are received, the report can be revised using your best judgments about what to use and what to ignore.

Short reports are most likely to be read. Teachers may be most interested in things that pertain to them or their role in the program. A one-page summary hitting the high points of the evaluation—what was evaluated, the purpose of the evaluation, major findings (strengths and weaknesses), and recommendations—may best fit the needs of many stakeholders.

A useful guide to communicating evaluation results is the following source:

Torres, R., Preskill, H. S., & Piontek, M. E. (1996). *Evaluation strategies for communicating and reporting*. Thousand Oaks, CA: Sage.

USING THE RESULTS
OF A PROGRAM EVALUATION

One of the fundamental principles of program evaluation is that the evaluation should not be done if it is not going to be used. It is a waste of scarce resources to invest time in an evaluation that sits on a shelf or receives no follow-up. So, assuming that the program evaluation will be used, you need to consider how it will be used and how you can facilitate its use. As noted in Chapter 1, the evaluators should consider the many payoffs of program evaluation. How could the program evaluation be used to improve the school program?

FOLLOW-UPS TO THE EVALUATION

First, target the program evaluation report to the use(s) where it will do the most good for the school building. Then, make a commitment to help other program staff use the evaluation results. Finally, assist other staff in reviewing the results and translating them into a plan of action that will then be implemented. A follow-up evaluation may then determine whether the actions taken have strengthened the program. The plan of action for the program might include plans to keep the district administration and the public informed and may also be used as a basis for planning staff development for the program staff.

This chapter can be summarized by the following key points:

1. Identify the audiences that should receive information about the program.
2. Choose an appropriate method to report findings to each audience.
3. Follow up to see that the evaluation findings are translated into an appropriate plan of action.

Illustrative Case Study (Part 5)

Mr. Henry anticipated some real interest in the findings of the science evaluation, not only from teachers but also from parents and the school board. They knew about the evaluation and naturally would be curious about the results.

In December, Mr. Henry called a meeting of the steering committee to discuss who should receive what information using what means of communication. The other teachers at Johnson Elementary School and Mrs. Goss were obvious audiences, but the committee decided to prepare a report to parents and to the school board as well. Miss Radisson then frowned reflectively and said, "You know, the superintendent will need to approve anything we send to parents or the school board. We'd better include her as an audience, too."

"Good idea," agreed Mr. Henry.

"The middle school principals might want to share our recommendations with their science teachers, too," said Mr. Williams. "And come to think of it, I'll bet the other elementary schools would be interested in what we're planning. We should include the elementary principals as an audience."

"Right on. Now, should we use the same report for all audiences?" asked Mr. Henry.

After some discussion, the committee decided to use a question-and-answer format for Mrs. Goss and the other teachers at Johnson Elementary School. Each evaluation question would be followed by tables, qualitative findings, interpretations, and recommendations. The purposes, procedures, and recommendations would be written as a brief executive summary for interested parents, the school board, and personnel in the other buildings. Availability of the summary would be announced to parents through the school district newsletter. If any of these audiences wanted more details, they would be sent a copy of the results reported to Mrs. Goss and the Johnson Elementary School teachers.

The members also agreed that a time schedule for implementing the recommendations would be part of the report going to Mrs. Goss and the Johnson teachers. Before any report went out, however, they further agreed that a draft would be reviewed by Mrs. Goss and anyone she would want to involve. They wanted to make sure that the reports were accurate and clear. They were also open to suggestions for improving the recommendations and the implementation plan.

The final chapter of this guide provides information on the administration of a program evaluation.

6

ADMINISTERING
THE EVALUATION

A program evaluation can be fairly complex. The logistics can be overwhelming at times, time schedules can place a burden on all who are involved, budgets need to be watched, and colleagues will need supervision and guidance. Then, there are the politics of the school; interpersonal relationships to nurture; the communication needs of participants; ethical considerations; and, of course, the unforeseen. Dealing with all of this takes a well-organized person or group and a good management plan. It also takes some flexibility, tolerance for ambiguity, and a sense of humor. This is no small order.

DEVELOPING A MANAGEMENT
PLAN FOR THE EVALUATION

In Chapter 3, details of a science program evaluation were worked out on a set of sample worksheets (Figure 2.2). From the second set of worksheets (Figure 3.1 and Table 3.1), you can develop a list of assignments and a budget.

To establish assignments, first make a list of the different people listed in the worksheets, then indicate across calendar months how much of each person's time will be required. Using information from Table 3.1, personnel needs (number of days for each month) could be summarized as shown in Table 6.1.

TABLE 6.1   Sample Management Plan for the Evaluation

Personnel	Month												
	Aug	Sept	Oct	Nov	Dec	Jan	Feb	Mar	Apr	May	June	July	Aug
Evaluation Coordinator		1	1	6	2	4	8	2	1	1	15		
Typist		1		2			1		5				
Evaluation Committee											5		

The budget is also based on the worksheets for the illustrative case study: BUDGET

Duplication	$450
Postage	25
Materials	25
Total	$500

These figures are the totals of those found in Table 3.1. Because school staff are already being paid for their time, personnel time does not reflect new costs to the school district. Rather, these are already-paid-for resources that are being reassigned to do the evaluation.

Finally, a time schedule needs to be developed, again based on the illustra-   TIME
tive case study worksheets. There are two types of time charts commonly   SCHEDULES
used in program evaluation. The first is called a *Gantt chart*; it is used to plot evaluation activities (tasks) across the time period planned for the project. This type of chart helps to visualize when peak busy times will occur. The Gantt chart developed by Mr. Henry in the illustrative case study is shown in Figure 6.1.

A second type of time chart is called an *activity network*. It plots activities and milestones along the way to the end product. This chart helps to visualize those activities that can go on simultaneously and those that are dependent on earlier activities. Like the Gantt chart, it can also be used to monitor progress on the evaluation to ensure that things are getting done on time. The activity network developed by Mr. Henry (using the example of Table 3.1) is presented in Figure 6.2.

These management tools will help the evaluation coordinator keep on schedule and within budget. Alone, however, they will not guarantee a successful project. Careful monitoring of the quality of work, cooperation by staff, needs for revising the project plan, and needs to adapt to unforeseen events should also occupy your mind.

POLITICS, ETHICS, AND THE INTERPERSONAL ASPECTS OF PROGRAM EVALUATION

Evaluation is a human activity, and it is accompanied by interesting forms of human behavior. The politics of evaluation produce undue pressure on the evaluator or participants in the evaluation. Forms of this pressure are lack of cooperation, attempts to derail the evaluation, attempts to discredit it, or attempts to influence its outcome(s). It is hard to foresee when, if ever, political influences may appear, but there are some things that evaluators can do to minimize their role.

Figure 6.1. Gantt Chart for Program Evaluation

Evaluation Question	Activity	Month												
		Aug	Sep	Oct	Nov	Dec	Jan	Feb	Mar	Apr	May	Jun	Jul	Aug
1.	a. Create survey form	//////												
	b. Survey teachers		//////											
	c. Compile results			//////										
	d. Get comments				////									
	e. Compare to curriculum					////								
	r. Committee review										//////			
	g. Prepare report										//////			
2.	a. Create survey form								//////					
	b. Survey teachers									//////				
	c. Compile survey results										////			
	d. Compile test results							//////						
	e. Committee review											///		
	f. Prepare report											///		
3-4.	a. Create teacher survey form				////									
	b. Survey teachers					///								
	c. Compile results						//////							
	d. Committee review											//////		
	e. Prepare report											///		
5.	a. Compile standards			//////////										
	b. Compare curriculum to standards					//////////								
	c. Summarize strengths and weaknesses					//////////								
	d. Prepare report											//////		

Figure 6.2. Activity Network for Program Evaluation

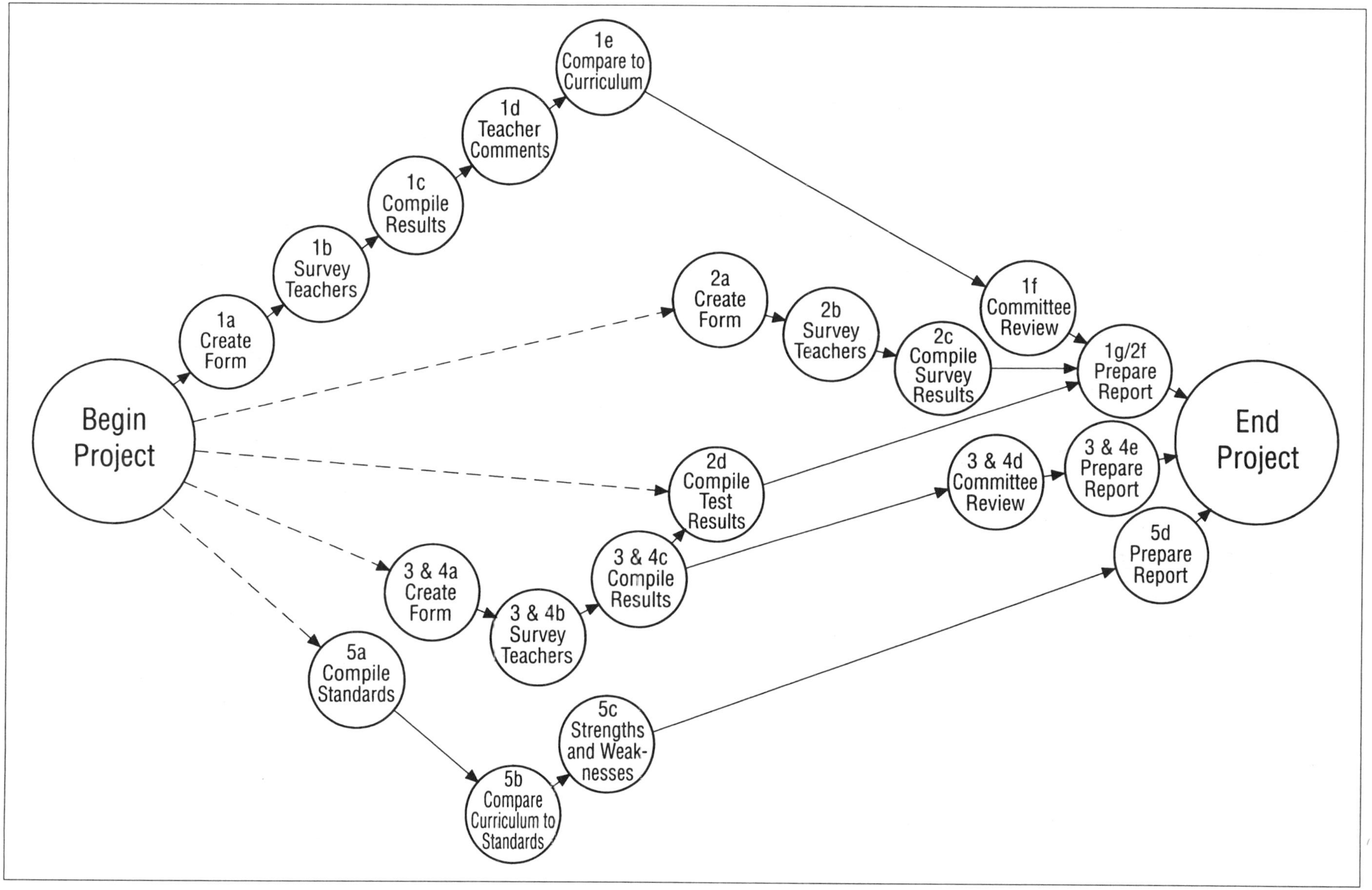

DEALING WITH   1. Establish and maintain open communications among evaluators
SCHOOL POLITICS   and stakeholders.

2. Anticipate political pressures and try to meet them head on through
   private meetings or, if that does not work, assistance from a supervi-
   sor.

3. Involve in the evaluation all individuals or groups who may have a
   vested interest in its outcomes.

4. Have frequent meetings and informal chats to keep people informed about the evaluation and to enlist their support.

5. Write the report carefully and submit a draft for review comments to
   key stakeholders.

ETHICAL   The ethics of evaluation are a concern when one considers the way in which
CONSIDERATIONS   participants are treated. If confidential records or other information are col-
                 lected, the evaluators are bound to protect that confidentiality, usually by
                 keeping data under lock and key. Participants need to be protected from
                 embarrassment or harassment. Individuals should not be identified in re-
                 ports unless they give permission. They should be treated with diplomacy
                 and respect; they should not be subjected to any form of physical or psycho-
                 logical harm or even potential for harm. If data are being collected from stu-
                 dents, most school districts have policies about parental permission. You
                 need to remain aboveboard and neutral in the collection of information and
                 the making of recommendations. You must honor promises and commit-
                 ments. You must also be incorruptible, reporting any possible conflicts of
                 interest or attempts to influence the outcomes of the evaluation. This is a
                 tall order, but given the stake that many people have in the results of a pro-
                 gram evaluation, trust and credibility are essential ingredients to a success-
                 ful evaluation.

                 A useful reference in this case is the following source:

                 Newman, D. L., & Brown, R. D. (1996). *Applied ethics for program evaluation.*
                 Thousand Oaks, CA: Sage.

INTERPERSONAL   Interpersonal relationships can be strained if the evaluator is demanding,
RELATIONS   undiplomatic, or insensitive to the feelings of others. Protocol violations
                 will also lead to interpersonal strain. You should make every effort to un-
                 derstand the views of participants and to honor them. Evaluators should be
                 good listeners, especially about the evaluation, and maintain good commu-
                 nications about the evaluation with participants. Evaluators should also
                 avoid disruption of routines and work schedules to the greatest extent pos-
                 sible.

This chapter can be summarized by the following key points:

1. Develop a management plan for the evaluation that details assignments, a budget, and a time schedule.
2. Attend to the political, ethical, and interpersonal dimensions of the evaluation from beginning to end.

Illustrative Case Study (Part 6)

With most of the details of the evaluation study worked out, Mr. Henry has pulled them together into an effective management plan. As he reflects on the careful planning that has gone into the evaluation of Johnson Elementary School's science program, he cannot help but feel secure about the rest of the study. Having a detailed road map makes the job much easier and allows him to be comfortable with the knowledge that he now really does know what he is doing.

Mr. Henry can also attend to what many consider the small things in program evaluation, the items that he knows can become big things if left unattended. Fortunately, he is in a school where people work well together and there is not a lot of resistance to change. He will, however, walk the hallways and chat with colleagues about the science evaluation. He will keep his sensors out and attempt to address any potential problems before they become real.

"This evaluation business is getting to be fun," he thinks as he walks down the hallway. He cannot help but feel pleased about all that he is learning about elementary-level science education and about knowing that what he and the steering committee do this year will have consequences for Lakeview City's youth for years to come.

Epilogue

This guide started with the statement that there are two things one should remember about evaluating programs in education. First, not everyone will see the program in the same light, and this pluralism should be reflected in the program evaluation report. Second, attend to three characteristics of good program evaluation—communication, communication, and communication. Having completed the six chapters of this guide, you should have a better understanding and appreciation for the basis of these statements. It is time now to put these guidelines into practice.

The Joint Committee on Standards for Education Evaluation, a coalition of 16 professional organizations concerned with the quality of evaluations in education, has published program evaluation standards. These standards may be used to assess the quality of any program evaluation. A summary of the standards appears in Resource C.

THE JOINT COMMITTEE STANDARDS

Resource A:
Annotated Bibliography
on Program Evaluation

Bloom, B. S., Hastings, J. T., & Madaus, G. F. (1971). *Handbook of formative and summative evaluation of student learning.* New York: McGraw-Hill.

This reference work contains separate chapters on the assessment of student learning in each of the following subject areas: preschool education, early language development, language arts, secondary social studies, art, science, secondary mathematics, literature, writing, learning in a second language, and industrial education. Chapters are also dedicated to techniques for assessing achievement of affective and different levels of cognitive objectives.

Herman, J. L. (Ed.). (1987). *Program evaluation kit* (2nd ed.). Newbury Park, CA: Sage.

This collection is a practical guide to the entire evaluation process, from evaluation design to reporting. The kit includes handy tips, exercises, data collection forms, flowcharts, graphs, measurement instruments, and other illustrative items. The nine volumes in the kit are as follows: *Evaluator's Handbook* (Vol. 1), *How to Focus an Evaluation* (Vol. 2), *How to Design a Program Evaluation* (Vol. 3), *How to Use Qualitative Methods in Evaluation* (Vol. 4), *How to Assess Program Implementation* (Vol. 5), *How to Measure Attitudes* (Vol. 6), *How to Measure Performance and Use Tests* (Vol. 7), *How to Analyze Data* (Vol. 8), and *How to Communicate Evaluation Findings* (Vol. 9).

Hopkins, K. D. (1998). *Educational and psychological measurement and evaluation* (8th ed.). Boston: Allyn & Bacon.

One of the best available references for constructing achievement tests, this textbook also provides readable explanations of the concepts of measurement validity and reliability. Chapters on standardized aptitude, achievement, interest, and social measures provide a useful overview of available standardized instruments.

Jaeger, R. M. (1990). *Statistics: A spectator sport* (2nd ed.). Newbury Park, CA: Sage.

This book is for those who want to develop an understanding of the use and interpretation of statistics commonly used in education. It contains clear explanations and many practical examples in the areas of measures of central tendency and variability, correlation, and hypothesis testing when comparing group averages.

Joint Committee on Standards for Education Evaluation. (1994). *The program evaluation standards.* Thousand Oaks, CA: Sage.

How do you know if a program evaluation has been planned or done well? Apply the joint committee's standards to the design or final report. This listing of 30 standards for program evaluation is the authoritative reference on principles of good program evaluation. Sponsored by 16 professional associations concerned with the quality of program evaluations in education, the joint committee has defined state-of-the-art principles, guidelines, and illustrative cases that can be used to judge the quality of any program evaluation. The standards fall into four categories with regard to the evaluation: utility, feasibility, propriety, and accuracy (see Resource C).

United Way of America. (1996). *Measuring program outcomes.* Alexandria, VA: Author.

This guide provides a very practical step-by-step overview of the process of developing logic models and then using them to design outcome measures as part of the program evaluation process. This guide is used throughout the United States for training evaluators in outcomes measurement.

Worthen, B. R., Sanders, J. R., & Fitzpatrick, J. L. (1997). *Program evaluation.* New York: Longman.

This text is divided into five sections. The first covers the theoretical, historical, and philosophical foundations of program evaluation. The second provides descriptions of alternative approaches to program evaluation. The third and fourth provide practical guidelines for planning, conducting, and using program evaluations. The practical guidelines cover clarifying the evaluation request and responsibilities; setting boundaries and analyzing the evaluation context; identifying and selecting the evaluative questions, criteria, and issues; planning information collection, analysis, and interpretation; developing a management plan; dealing with political, ethical, and interpersonal aspects of evaluation; reporting and using evaluation information; and evaluating evaluations. The fifth addresses emerging and future settings for program evaluation. A case study example runs through the practical guidelines sections.

RESOURCE B:
TAXONOMY OF
COGNITIVE OBJECTIVES

A. Knowledge
    1. Specifics
    2. Ways and means of dealing with specifics
    3. Universals and abstractions

B. Comprehension
    1. Translation
    2. Interpretation
    3. Extrapolation

C. Application

D. Analysis
    1. Elements
    2. Relationships
    3. Organizational principles

E. Synthesis
    1. Unique communication
    2. Plan
    3. Derivations

F. Evaluation
    1. Using internal evidence
    2. Using external criteria

Resource C:
Standards for
Program Evaluations

These standards have been established by the Joint Committee on Standards for Education Evaluation:

UTILITY STANDARDS

The utility standards are intended to ensure that an evaluation will serve the information needs of intended users.

U1   Stakeholder Identification

Persons involved in or affected by the evaluation should be identified, so that their needs can be addressed.

U2   Evaluator Credibility

The persons conducting the evaluation should be both trustworthy and competent to perform the evaluation, so that the evaluation findings achieve maximum credibility and acceptance.

U3   Information Scope and Selection

Information collected should be broadly selected to address pertinent questions about the program and be responsive to the needs and interests of clients and other specified stakeholders.

U4   Values Identification

The perspectives, procedures, and rationale used to interpret the findings should be carefully described, so that the bases for value judgments are clear.

U5   Report Clarity

Evaluation reports should clearly describe the program being evaluated, including its context, and the purposes, procedures, and findings of the evaluation, so that essential information is provided and easily understood.

U6   Report Timeliness and Dissemination

Significant interim findings and evaluation reports should be disseminated to intended users, so that they can be used in a timely fashion.

U7   Evaluation Impact

Evaluations should be planned, conducted, and reported in ways that encourage follow-through by stakeholders, so that the likelihood that the evaluation will be used is increased.

FEASIBILITY

The feasibility standards are intended to ensure that an evaluation will be realistic, prudent, diplomatic, and frugal.

F1   Practical Procedures

The evaluation procedures should be practical, to keep disruption to a minimum while needed information is obtained.

F2   Political Viability

The evaluation should be planned and conducted with anticipation of the different positions of various interest groups, so that their cooperation may be obtained, and so that possible attempts by any of these groups to curtail evaluation operations or to bias or misapply the results can be averted or counteracted.

F3   Cost-Effectiveness

The evaluation should be efficient and produce information of sufficient value, so that the resources expended can be justified.

PROPRIETY

The propriety standards are intended to ensure that an evaluation will be conducted legally, ethically, and with due regard for the welfare of those involved in the evaluation as well as those affected by its results.

P1   Service Orientation

Evaluations should be designed to assist organizations to address and effectively serve the needs of the full range of targeted participants.

P2   Formal Agreements

Obligations of the formal parties to an evaluation (what is to be done, how, by whom, when) should be agreed to in writing, so that these parties are obligated to adhere to all conditions of the agreement or formally to renegotiate it.

P3   Rights of Human Subjects

Evaluations should be designed and conducted to respect and protect the rights and welfare of human subjects.

P4   Human Interactions

Evaluators should respect human dignity and worth in their interactions with other persons associated with an evaluation, so that participants are not threatened or harmed.

P5   Complete and Fair Assessment

The evaluation should be complete and fair in its examination and recording of strengths and weaknesses of the program being evaluated, so that strengths can be built upon and problem areas addressed.

P6   Disclosure of Findings

The formal parties to an evaluation should ensure that the full set of evaluation findings along with pertinent limitations are made accessible to the persons affected by the evaluation and any others with expressed legal rights to receive the results.

P7   Conflict of Interest

Conflict of interest should be dealt with openly and honestly, so that it does not compromise the evaluation processes and results.

P8   Fiscal Responsibility

The evaluator's allocation and expenditure of resources should reflect sound accountability procedures and otherwise be prudent and ethically responsible, so that expenditures are accounted for and appropriate.

ACCURACY

The accuracy standards are intended to ensure that an evaluation will reveal and convey technically adequate information about the features that determine worth of merit of the program being evaluated.

A1   Program Documentation

The program being evaluated should be described and documented clearly and accurately so that the program is clearly identified.

A2   Context Analysis

The context in which the program exists should be examined in enough detail so that its likely influences on the program can be identified.

A3   Described Purposes and Procedures

The purposes and procedures of the evaluation should be monitored and described in enough detail so that they can be identified and assessed.

A4   Defensible Information Sources

The sources of information used in a program evaluation should be described in enough detail so that the adequacy of the information can be assessed.

A5   Valid Information

The information-gathering procedures should be chosen or developed and then implemented so that they will ensure that the interpretation arrived at is valid for the intended use.

A6   Reliable Information

The information-gathering procedures should be chosen or developed and then implemented so that they will ensure that the information obtained is sufficiently reliable for the intended use.

A7   Systematic Information

The information collected, processed, and reported in an evaluation should be systematically reviewed and any errors found should be corrected.

A8   Analysis of Quantitative Information

Quantitative information in an evaluation should be appropriately and systematically analyzed so that evaluation questions are effectively answered.

A9   Analysis of Qualitative Information

Qualitative information in an evaluation should be appropriately and systematically analyzed so that evaluation questions are effectively answered.

A10   Justified Conclusions

The conclusions reached in an evaluation should be explicitly justified, so that stakeholders can assess them.

A11   Impartial Reporting

Reporting procedures should guard against distortion caused by personal feelings and biases of any party to the evaluation so that evaluation reports fairly reflect the evaluation findings.

A12   Metaevaluation

The evaluation itself should be formatively and summatively evaluated against these and other pertinent standards so that its conduct is appropriately guided and, on completion, stakeholders can closely examine its strengths and weaknesses.

Guidelines and illustrative cases to assist evaluation participants in meeting each of these standards are provided in *The Program Evaluation Standards* (Joint Committee on Standards for Education Evaluation, 1994). The illustrative cases are based in a variety of educational settings, including schools, universities, medical and health care fields, the military, business and industry, the government, and law.

References

Airasian, P. W. (1997). *Classroom assessment.* New York: McGraw-Hill.

Bloom, B. S., Englehart, M. D., Furst, E. J., Hill, W. H., & Krathwohl, D. R. (1956). *Taxonomy of educational objectives. Handbook 1: Cognitive domain.* New York: David McKay.

Bloom, B. S., Hastings, J. T., & Madaus, G. F. (1971). *Handbook of formative and summative evaluation of student learning.* New York: McGraw-Hill.

Budd, R. W., Thop, R. K., & Donohew, L. (1967). *Content analysis of communication.* New York: Macmillan.

Denzin, N. K., & Lincoln, Y. S. (Eds.). (1994). *Handbook of qualitative research.* Thousand Oaks, CA: Sage.

Dillman, D. A. (1978). *Mail and telephone surveys: The total design method.* New York: John Wiley.

Fink, A. (1995). *The Survey Kit.* Thousand Oaks, CA: Sage.

Fink, A., & Kosecoff, J. (1998). *How to conduct surveys* (2nd ed.). Thousand Oaks, CA: Sage.

Fowler, F. J., Jr. (1989). *Survey research methods* (2nd ed.). Newbury Park, CA: Sage.

Fowler, F. J., Jr., & Mangione, T. W. (1990). *Standardized survey interviewing: Minimizing interviewer-related error.* Newbury Park, CA: Sage.

Gall, M. D., Borg, W. R., & Gall, J. P. (1996). *Educational research* (6th ed.). New York: Longman.

Gordon, R. L. (1980). *Interviewing: Strategy, techniques, and tactics.* Homewood, IL: Dorsey.

Guba, E. G., & Lincoln, Y. S. (1981). *Effective evaluation.* San Francisco: Jossey-Bass.

Herman, J. L. (Ed.). (1987). *Program evaluation kit* (2nd ed.). Newbury Park, CA: Sage.

Holsti, O. (1969). *Content analysis for the social sciences and humanities.* Reading, MA: Addison-Wesley.

Hopkins, K. D. (1998). *Educational and psychological measurement and evaluation* (8th ed.). Boston: Allyn & Bacon.

Hopkins, K. D., Hopkins, B. R., & Glass, G. V. (1996). *Basic statistics for the behavioral sciences* (3rd ed.). Boston: Allyn & Bacon.

Jaeger, R. M. (1990). *Statistics: A spectator sport* (2nd ed.). Newbury Park, CA: Sage.

Joint Committee on Standards for Education Evaluation. (1994). *The program evaluation standards*. Thousand Oaks, CA: Sage.

Metfessel, N. S., & Michael, W. B. (1967). A paradigm involving multiple criterion measures for the evaluation of the effectiveness of school programs. *Educational and Psychological Measurement, 27*, 931-943.

Newman, D. L., & Brown, R. D. (1996). *Applied ethics for program evaluation*. Thousand Oaks, CA: Sage.

Robinson, J. P., Shaver, P. R., & Wrightsman, L. S. (Eds.). (1991). *Measures of personality and social psychological attitudes*. New York: Academic Press.

Shaw, M. R., & Wright, J. M. (1967). *Scales for measurement of attitudes*. New York: McGraw-Hill.

Simon, A., & Boyer, E. G. (1974). *Mirrors of behavior: An anthology of observation instruments*. Philadelphia: Research for Better Schools.

Stufflebeam, D. L. (1969). Evaluation as enlightenment for decision making. In W. A. Beaty (Ed.), *Improving assessment and an inventory of measures of affective behavior*. Washington, DC: Association for Supervision and Curriculum Development.

Torres, R., Preskill, H. S., & Piontek, M. E. (1996). *Evaluation strategies for communicating and reporting*. Thousand Oaks, CA: Sage.

United Way of America. (1996). *Measuring program outcomes*. Alexandria, VA: Author.

Webb, E. J., Campbell, D. T., Schwartz, R. D., & Sechrest, L. (1966). *Unobtrusive measures: Nonreactive research in the social sciences*. Chicago: Rand McNally.

Worthen, B. R., Sanders, J. R., & Fitzpatrick, J. L. (1997). *Program evaluation*. New York: Longman.

INDEX